The Pornography Trap

Setting Pastors and Laypersons Free from Sexual Addiction

Ralph H. Earle Jr. and Mark R. Laaser

Beacon Hill Press of Kansas City
Kansas City, Missouri

Copyright 2002
by Beacon Hill Press of Kansas City

ISBN: 083-411-9382

Printed in the United States of America

Cover Design: Isaac Abundis

10   9   8   7   6   5   4   3   2   1

Contents

Introduction   5

1. "A Funny Thing Happened on the
   Way to Seminary"   11

2. Pastoral Vulnerability   23

3. Wounds   35

4. Healthy Sexuality   45

5. The Physical Dimension   55

6. The Behavioral Dimension   67

7. The Emotional Dimension   81

8. The Relational Dimension, Part One   95

9. The Relational Dimension, Part Two   109

10. Spiritual Healing   125

Notes   135

Resources   139

Introduction

Peter grew up in a small Midwestern town in the 1950s. He gave his heart to Christ at a Billy Graham campaign and almost immediately felt called to the ministry. Sexual activity was almost always important to Peter. He had masturbated at least once a day since he was 13—starting when he discovered his dad's adult magazine. Sometimes he masturbated two or more times a day, especially when he felt lonely or his parents were arguing. Masturbation became his release from tension during his high school years.

Peter went to a Christian college and fell in love with Doris. During college, Peter and Doris became involved in heavy petting, though they never had physical intercourse. They were saving themselves for marriage. Peter continued to masturbate regularly and then discovered X-rated movies on TV and sex phone lines. No one knew Peter was involved in these activities.

After college graduation, Peter married Doris and decided to attend seminary. During their first months together, the two of them were very busy and happy. Doris taught school, and Peter attended seminary and worked as a part-time youth minister. A couple of times Doris thought Peter was flirting with a senior high girl, but decided she was probably imagining things. However, her worst fear was confirmed when Peter was called into the senior pastor's office—two sets of parents had complained that Peter had kissed their daughters.

Peter confessed to his boss and to his wife that he was indeed guilty. He was required to take a leave of absence and to take at least one quarter of Clinical Pastoral Education and to get some individual and marriage therapy. During his therapy time with Doris, Peter disclosed his history of inappropriate sexual behavior. Doris was shocked.

Unfortunately this type of story is repeated behind the closed doors of many of our parsonage homes.

Most of us are painfully aware that an epidemic fills our churches today. Pornography is a virus affecting the heart and soul of Christian leadership. Some of you know other colleagues who are affected. Some of you are plagued yourselves. A recent

Leadership Journal survey indicated that almost one-third of all pastors struggle with Internet pornography.

Internet pornography is the new kid on the block, but it is only one challenge to the pastor in the 21st century. The Internet has made pornography more accessible, affordable, and seemingly anonymous. The horror of being discovered by a spouse or church secretary—or even more damaging, by a child—is immense.

That type of a scenario is regularly being enacted in the lives of Christian clergy throughout the world. No denomination is exempt. It is an interfaith crisis! The stories about clergy having sexual encounters with church members, staff, and people outside the church are rapidly increasing. This does not necessarily mean that the numbers of sexual encounters are increasing. Certainly more media attention has highlighted this problem, and many more victims are telling their stories.

This is certainly not a new phenomenon. The Bible tells us about Samson visiting prostitutes and having a relationship with Delilah. Samson is depicted as the strongest man in the Bible. But the Bible clearly shows who had the upper hand when it came to physical prowess.

Pastors who give away their power to pornography can understand Samson's weakness and lust—which led to the loss of his spiritual commitment, his power, his eyes, and his freedom. This book contains such stories that reflect the real-life scenarios many pastors live. Most of these real-life stories remain hidden, providing deep fear and enormous guilt. Probably the most frequently told story about the destructive power of sexual sin is that of David. David was a popular king whose affair with Bathsheba (2 Sam. 11:1—12:25) highlighted his decline. Trying to hide his sexual indiscretion, he eventually had Bathsheba's husband, Uriah, murdered.

We, the authors, have not dealt with a pastor who has resorted to assassination in order to keep a secret. However, too many times the use of pornography, combined with masturbation, leads to acute depression and suicidal temptations.

Solomon may have been a very wise man. Yet he could not have envisioned many centuries later a pastor reading, "Your two breasts are like two fawns, like twin fawns of a gazelle that browse among the lilies" (Song of Songs 4:5). Thus a pastor does not have to go to an adult bookstore or access the Internet to read something that can become pornographic to someone who is out of control sexually. Paul, who lived at a time of blatant sexual immorality, admonishes the Bible's readers to be sexually pure—especially the leaders of the church.

Church history is replete with examples of fallen church leadership. Sexual sin is interfaith and crosses the centuries.

Today, many churches struggle with the fallout of a pastor whose sexual indiscretions have been discovered. The media accounts will continue to mount as more pastors' stories become public. In some states it is a felony for a pastor to have sex with a parishioner. The pendulum has swung from very few ethical codes surrounding sexual conduct with parishioners to extensive written information and training sessions about sex in the workplace for clergy. Both authors are themselves used extensively not only to treat those in need but also to talk to church groups about prevention and preventive policies.

In this book we shall attempt to answer some basic questions:

- What is the nature of this enormous crisis and challenge to the church?
- What can pastors do to minimize their vulnerability in this area?
- What are some of the risk factors for clergy, and how can we identify them?
- How can our pastors enjoy healthy sexual experiences for themselves and their spouses?

What does the Bible have to say about sexuality?

In Rom. 12:2 Paul tells us not to conform to the ways of the world but to "be transformed by the renewing of [our minds]." We can identify with any pastor who finds that difficult to do. We will give specific suggestions learned through our own pain and the pain of those we have treated. Mark Laaser writes as a pastor who experienced sexual addiction and lost his ministry as a result in 1987.

You may have your own stories in this area. So first read this book as an audit of your own life. For many clergy this may be a reversal of the usual procedure. Matt. 7:3 succinctly says, "Why do you look at the speck of sawdust in your brother's eye and pay no attention to the plank in your own eye?"

As you read the following chapters, we encourage you to pay attention to any understandings that may apply to your life. An example is the story of a pastor who was a workaholic and did not have balance in his life. George graduated from seminary 15 years ago. He used to love his work and felt called by God. During the last couple of years he felt some anger toward some members of his church. He did not feel comfortable discussing his feelings with anyone. There was a lot of tension in his marriage. His wife believed that he put the church ahead of his family. Thus he discovered that if he talked to her about his frustration, they argued about his priorities.

George had a charismatic personality. One afternoon while on his computer, he stumbled onto a pornographic site and decided to explore it for a couple of minutes. He was shocked when he realized that he had spent nearly two hours viewing pornography on the Internet. He wound up masturbating, then felt guilty and frightened. He fell to his knees and promised God he would never go to the Internet pornographic sites again. The next week during sermon preparation, he did the same thing. Again he prayed about it and thought that God had forgiven him and that he would not repeat this. To his dismay the behavior not only continued but also progressed to a daily ritual. One of his greatest fears came true when his wife woke one night and came into his study. She was horrified to see the computer showing two adults having intercourse. George was ashamed to have his secret revealed. Nothing in seminary had prepared him for this.

Neither George nor his wife slept well that night—both felt isolated and lonely. Neither knew whom to turn to for help. Now their marriage was in a huge crisis.

Paul wrote in Rom. 12:1, "Therefore, I urge you, brothers [and sisters], in view of God's mercy, to offer your bodies as living sacrifices, holy and pleasant to God—this is your spiritual act of worship." What a powerful scriptural injunction. We interpret this text as, "Present your eyes to God so that what you view on the Internet is acceptable to God." That statement is for those who have a need and have ears to hear. It integrates well the biblical message with the current crisis in the church. As pastors we must never forget that we are earthen vessels who, in our finiteness, are vulnerable to be both the victim and victimizer of sexual sin.

There is a long history of pastors who are unlikely to be alcoholics but are susceptible to the drug of sex. Many sex addicts will state that sex is their primary addiction, even though they may also be addicted to alcohol or some substance. Unfortunately the

Adam and Eve story of the lure of the forbidden fruit is a dynamic that most pastors understand personally and is dramatically clear to the pastor who finds pornography.

Cybersex and the entire world of electronic communications open a vast access for pastors to pornography. Every church leader, minister, and religious educator faces challenges in this area. We will look at the areas of sexual arousal, sexual exploitation, and healthy and unhealthy romantic impulses. We will also give the pastor options for dealing with them. The great technological boom of the Internet has provided terror for many pastors.

The good news is that the current crisis with Internet pornography is forcing many pastors to evaluate deeper emotional and spiritual issues in their lives. All forms of addiction, sexual and otherwise, can be traced to problems with intimacy—intimacy with God and with each other.

Ralph Earle was one of the first to describe this dynamic as being "intimacy able" or "intimacy disabled." This book will describe the sexual sin of pornography, the "pornography trap," but will also look at other forms of sexual sinfulness. All sin can be progressive, and the wages of it can be death. We cannot stress enough that looking at pornography, however harmless it may seem at first, is like this. It will probably get worse over time and could even lead to deadly consequences.

We will look at how some clergy have even become sex offenders in the criminal definition of that term. We will discuss how many pastors get to the point where pornography becomes a problem. We will examine family-of-origin, cultural, work, marital and family issues; imbalances in lifestyle; and other relevant aspects of the complex nature of etiology. New research is teaching a lot about the neurological architecture of sex. We will look at some of the most recent data regarding this dynamic.

We recently heard Dr. H. B. London of *Focus on the Family* speak to pastors citing the numerous biblical passages that challenge us to "flee" from sin, the dangers of this world. We all must flee from sin, but those who are caught already in the trap of pornography will have to know escape routes. The good news is that the answer does lie in spiritual recovery and that tools are available that can make a difference in a pastor's life and family. Much of this book is devoted to understanding healthy sexuality as being a large part of the answer.

If pornography is a challenge for you, we suggest you read the following chapters carefully and prayerfully. We are pastors, so we write to you as brothers. At times you will need to put this book down and talk to someone. We pray that you have safe people in your life to whom you can talk. There is hope. We pray that this book will be a blessing to you.

1

"A Funny Thing Happened on the Way to Seminary"

Bob is a successful pastor in a large Protestant denomination. He is married, with three children. His wife and he met at their denominational college, and each came from a family strong in its faith.

Since college days Bob has struggled with pornography and masturbation. He hoped that getting married would take away his "lust." He was shocked and disappointed that regular marital sex didn't stop him from looking at pornography and masturbating. Periodically, he would "repent" and try to stop these activities but would always return to them.

Over the years of his ministry, Bob has frequently rented pornographic videos. Recently, when the church obtained on-line access, Bob became fascinated with Internet pornography. He has also become preoccupied with the idea of going to a massage parlor.

In his first three churches, Bob became emotionally involved with several women in each church. In his current congregation, Bob's relationship with the organist has become sexual. Bob is depressed and is having difficulty performing his pastoral duties. He doesn't know who to talk to. And his wife wonders what is going on.

Bob is a pastor who got trapped in pornography and began to struggle with sexual addiction. In his addiction, problems with pornography became worse. Now Bob has committed several different kinds of sexual sin or sexual misconduct.

When he became sexual with a church staff member, Bob committed sexual abuse. Previously, he came dangerously close to sexually abusing members of his church. Bob's case began with a very basic pornography problem. He illustrates what can happen if the basic problem is not addressed early.

Bob's story does allow us to define some important distinctions between these three terms: "sexual addiction," "sexual sin and misconduct," and "sexual abuse." There is a great deal of confusion in the church about these distinctions. Some would assume, for example, that all sexual sin is addictive.

Dramatic cases of pastors sexually involved with church members have received a lot of media attention. While the percentages of pastors who sexually sin are very high, sexual sin does not automatically imply sexual addiction or sexually abusive behavior. Though we primarily want to speak to those who have struggled with basic forms of sexual sin, such as pornography, it is important to know the broad nature of sexual sin.

Sexual Addiction

The term "sexual addiction" came into use in the 1970s, when similarities were noticed in behavior between those who were out of control with repetitive sexual activity and alcoholics. Programs similar to Alcoholics Anonymous were started for sex addicts, and hospitals opened treatment programs.[1]

Sexual addiction has been defined as a pathological relationship to any form of sexual activity.[2] From a Christian perspective, pathological means any sex that is not the expression of spiritual and emotional intimacy between a couple. Pathological also means that sex is a substitute for, or an escape from, intimacy.

As an addiction, pathological sex becomes totally unmanageable. A sexual addict intends to stop but can't. Christians might think stopping sinful behavior is a matter of willpower. But sexual acting out is an expression of the addict's loneliness and anger. Part of this person is rebellious and feels entitled to get his or her needs met. So a sexual addict is at war with himself or herself. A part of the addict wants to stop, and another part doesn't.

Over time, the amount of sexual activity becomes progressively worse. Most sexual addicts can trace their addiction back to their adolescence and even childhood.

Getting worse does not always mean addicts will move to deeper levels of sin. But they will need either more of the same kind of activity or newer kinds of activity to produce the same result or "high." This factor is based on the brain's ability to adjust and is often called tolerance.

Sexual addiction is based on feelings of genuine sexual lust. "Lust" is a misunderstood word. Many Christians assume lust is inherently sinful. Lust, however, can be best understood as a feeling of desire. For any substance or behavior to be addictive it must involve the chemistry of the brain. Feelings of sexual pleasure and excitement involve this brain chemistry. Powerful neurochemical reactions are involved in very basic parts of the brain that create intense feelings of pleasure. If God had not built us this way, we would not procreate. It is a natural part of God's design.

Within itself the brain can get used to any level of neurochemical reaction. Over time, the brain needs more of this to achieve the same pleasure.

As with many addictions sexual feelings can be used to escape painful emotions. If the sexual activity is new, exciting, or dangerous, the adrenalin it brings can elevate an addict's mood. If the feelings are about romance, touching, being held, and the orgasmic experience of sex, powerful opiates in the brain can have a relaxing effect. If depressed, an addict can elevate his or her mood. If anxious or stressed, the person can depress his or her mood.

Sexual addiction usually leads to negative consequences. For pastors the consequences are often obvious. They may lose jobs or even their careers. Addicts can spend huge sums of money—we have known pastors who spend hundreds of thousands of dollars on sexual activity. One pastor, for example, spent $75,000 on the Internet in one month's time. Marriages are lost. Social and legal consequences can be severe. Pastors are arrested for everything from soliciting prostitution to sexual abuse. In some states it is a felony for a pastor to be sexual with a congregant. Pastors can also be sued in civil action for damages when they have had sex with congregation members. We even know a pastor who was arrested for stealing from banks to pay for prostitution. And physical consequences can be deadly. The incidence of STDs and even AIDS is profound.

Dr. Patrick Carnes says sex addicts are shame-based individuals who don't believe that anyone really knows or likes them or that anyone could possibly meet their needs. Sex becomes their most important need. For addicts, sexual activity, whether a fantasy or an actual encounter, symbolizes love and nurture. Carnes has also said that sex addicts are also very dependent, though they may act powerful.[3]

The shame and core beliefs of sexual addicts lead to a cycle of addiction that contains four stages:[4]

The first stage is engaging in fantasy, or a mental image of a

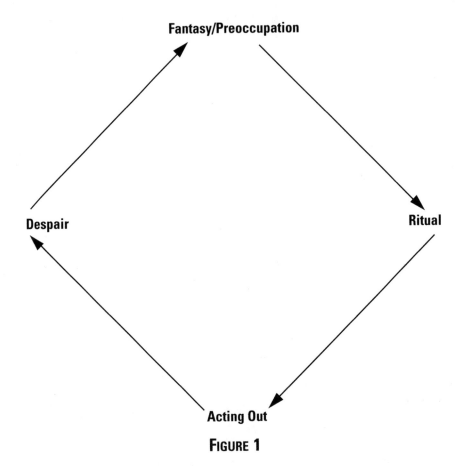

FIGURE 1

desired result. We can have many kinds of fantasies including athletic, financial, social, academic, and professional. Sexual and romantic fantasies are what we might consider to be ideal sexual or relationship situations. Fantasies are not abnormal. However, they become a problem when we become preoccupied with them. Sexual or relational fantasies usually involve images of the ideal people to be with. This may include their appearances, their behaviors, where the activities occur, and what happens sexually or romantically.

Fantasies alone can raise or lower moods. When we think of exciting or new situations, perhaps even dangerous situations, our moods can be elevated. When we think about warm and nurturing situations, our moods can be calmed. Fantasies contain emotional and spiritual longing. We long for nurture, affirmation, and touch.

Sometimes we long for control over past pain. Sometimes we long to express anger over our deep wounds. Fantasies have the potential in our minds to solve this pain.

Jesus said in Matt. 5:28 that even when we look at another person lustfully, we commit adultery. According to Scripture, fantasies are adulterous if we imagine any sexual or romantic relationship outside of marriage.

Fantasies lead to the next stage—ritual. Rituals are preparations a person makes to be sexual in a direct way. These preparations might be mental and practical.

An addict's preparations might include justifying the actions. Ministers tend to have very interesting ways to justify their behaviors. One of their most common justifications is the "martyr" excuse, in which they say, "I am such an overworked pastor. I take care of everyone else. No one takes care of me. I am underpaid. I deserve to get some needs met."

A minister may even gain the pity of others, and they become willing to do anything for him or her. A form of this excuse might be, "My spouse doesn't understand me, doesn't take care of me, doesn't fulfill my needs. What am I to do?" Ministers who use this excuse may even have a warped sense of, "If I do enough good for God and for others, God won't mind if I meet my needs."

> **Pornography, masturbation, and even prostitution seem harmless on the surface.**

Another rationalization is, "No one is getting hurt." These pastors think if no one really knows what is happening, no one is harmed. Pornography, masturbation, and even prostitution seem harmless on the surface. The mental and spiritual effects are never considered for very long. We have seen ministers who even thought affairs were not hurting anyone. If needy spouses come to them for help with a difficult marriage, these pastors even believe that they are being caring. Even the sexual relationship can be seen as "giving."

Another common excuse is a form of the martyr approach. These pastors think the world is so sexual in nature and that they were under such attack by evil influences, it was impossible to resist. These pastors may even preach against the evils of our culture. We are always a little suspicious of pastors who are so eloquent and so angry against the sinful evils of the world. It is as if they are preaching to themselves. It is also as if they are desperately hoping God will remove all sexual temptation from the world so they don't have to struggle.

When a pastor acts out with parishioners or others, this excuse goes so far as to blame the other person for being so aggressive. Sexual addicts and sexual sinners are good at blaming others for their actions.

When a pastor justifies sexual sin, he or she will next take steps to act (the third stage). These could be very simple steps. This person gets triggered into lustful fantasies, justifies acting out, and then privately looks at pornography and perhaps masturbates.

The steps can be even more elaborate. The pastor is out on pastoral calls and stops by an ATM at a bank. The hospital he is visiting is near a part of town with massage parlors. Since his time is his own and he is off doing God's work of visitation, no one will notice that he might be late getting home. He goes to the massage parlor.

Rituals leading to affairs can be very long. The pastor meets a person at church and is attracted. Over months, these two form a friendship, perhaps even around church business. They start having lunch, talk as friends, then share intimate details of their lives. Eventually they realize they are "soul mates." What are two star-crossed lovers to do but consummate this relationship? You might detect an element of anger in their, "Why didn't God let us find each other first?"

Since rituals are long and short, most pastors who struggle with this have more than one going on at the same time. They might have fantasies and thoughts, a pornography ritual, and several affairs with different people going on. At times they might "trade off" rituals for acting out. Such thinking goes like this, "I don't really want to have an affair, so today I will masturbate to control my temptations to do that."

This kind of thinking actually believes that to "only" masturbate is a complete moral victory because a more serious sin is avoided. By this we do not mean that masturbation as such is wrong or a sin. What is really important is whether or not it involves compulsive or obsessive acts that have a negative effect on a person's healthy sexuality and/or spirituality.

Sometimes just the excitement of the ritual is a form of acting out and can raise or lower mood. These rituals can take a profound amount of time and energy, as well as creative thinking and manipulations. The stage of acting out can involve any kind of sexual behavior leading to direct sexual expression.

Acting out always leads to the fourth stage—despair. The excitement has worn off, the thrill is gone, and conscience takes over. Carnes discovered that 71 percent of addicts have actually considered suicide in this stage.[5]

> **Many ministers medicate their pain with a religious workaholism.**

In this stage more promises are made, prayers said, and sometimes desperate actions taken to prevent acting out again. Some sex addicts harm themselves in this stage, such as the pornography addict who plucked out both eyes because Jesus said, "If your eye causes you to sin, pluck it out" (Mark 9:47).

At times addicts will turn to other substances or behaviors to medicate the feeling of despair. Many sex addicts suffer from other addictions such as alcoholism.[6] Many ministers medicate their pain with a religious workaholism. They may receive lots of affirmation for being so "faithful" and hardworking.

Sex addicts will eventually return to fantasies to medicate their loneliness. This is where the whole cycle started. The cycle spirals and usually gets more destructive over time.

In this section we have only touched the surface of sex addiction. Please know that what we have to say about the answer to the more general problem of sexual sin and temptation is the solution for sex addiction. There is hope. We know hundreds of men and women who have returned to sober and faithful lives.

Sexual Sin and Misconduct

While many clergy are sexually addicted, a far greater number sexually sin and commit sexual misconduct.[7] The terms "sexual sin" and "sexual misconduct" may refer to the same behavior. Christians might call something sin, while the secular world might call it misconduct. Sometimes what the Christian community considers immoral, the secular world does not.

Most pastors struggle with destructive fantasy, masturbation, pornography, or prostitution. Others may become involved in what the medical profession commonly refers to as *paraphilic* behaviors, many of which can become quite perverse and extreme. These might include exhibitionism, voyeurism, *fratteurism* (uninvited touch for the purpose of a sexual high), bestiality, obscene phone calls, and sadomasochistic behaviors. These sexual behaviors don't necessarily indicate addiction unless they're repetitive or out of control.

Sexual Abuse

The term "sexual abuse" assumes a person has used some form of control to be sexual with a person who is vulnerable to that power.

Power can take many forms. If a person uses physical power, rape results. What is less understood and accepted is the use of emotional or spiritual power. There are those who believe that anytime a pastor becomes sexual with a person that is subject to his or her influence as a pastor, it is a matter of "authority rape." This means a parishioner's trust has been violated and the damage done. This kind of sexual abuse has spiritual effects, so it is also spiritual abuse.

As we have said, some states have made it a felony when a pastor has sex with an adult in the church. This becomes confusing because on the surface some relationships appear consensual. The law now assumes that for the church member it is never consensual because of the power of the pastor's role.

Many studies have been done to describe the profile of therapists who abuse patients. But not much work has been done to describe pastors who abuse parishioners.

Since the roles of pastor and therapist have many similarities, let's look at some of these theories and see what they offer that might be relevant to pastors.

Remember, this problem of power abuse involves only a portion of those pastors who sexually sin. But this kind of problem receives much public attention and is a big problem in the church.

John Gonsiorek, who has diagnosed hundreds of therapist and clergy offenders, describes nine categories of sexual offenders.

1. The *naive offender* is ignorant of the ethics and unprepared to deal with the power differences in caregiving settings.

2. The *normal or mildly neurotic* professional may develop a gradual romantic relationship with a vulnerable person during a stressful time in his or her life.

3. The *severely neurotic or socially isolated* professional displays longer term personality traits such as depression, inadequacy, low self-esteem, and social isolation. This person may demonstrate a repetitive pattern of offending and will punish himself or herself rather than change behavior. This person has poor boundaries.

4. Professionals with *impulsive character disorders* practice a variety of inappropriate behavior, including even criminal acts and uninhibited behavior, but they are not cunning and don't plan actions.

5. *Sociopathic or narcissistic* personalities are more deliberate, cunning, and manipulative. They set out to offend more intentionally.

6. *Psychotics* demonstrate delusional thinking.

7. *"Classic" sex offenders* chronically and repeatedly offend. They include pedophiles or other types of sex offenders and may be impulsive and narcissistic.

8. The *medically disabled* experience mood disorder problems, especially bipolar disease (manic-depression), which carries a decided lack of moral judgment.

9. *Masochistic, self-defeating* individuals experience internal conflicts about setting boundaries. They increasingly give in to demanding and needy or vulnerable people.[8]

These categories academically help us understand sexual offenders. No pastor fits neatly into one of these categories. We find that pastors are rarely found in the last four categories (6-9). Those who prepare for ministry cannot usually pass screening procedures if they demonstrate the pathologies of these categories.

Glen Gabbard, of Menninger Clinic, Topeka, Kansas, describes four major types of offending professionals: (1) psychotic disorders, (2) predatory psychopathy and paraphilias, (3) lovesickness, and (4) masochistic surrender.

The two most common types of offenders among pastors are Nos. 2 and 3. Under lovesickness, Gabbard lists subcategories such as these: unconscious reenactment of incestuous longings; a wish for maternal nurturance; enactments of rescue fantasies; viewing clients as an idealized version of the self; confusion of therapist's own needs with the client's needs; fantasies that love is curative; repression of rage at the client's persistent thwarting of therapeutic efforts; anger at an authority; manic defense against mourning when ending counseling; the exception fantasy (I can get away with this!); insecurity about personal masculine identity; the client being seen as a transformational object; settling down by a female therapist of the "rowdy" male client; conflicts around sexual orientation.[9]

Marie Fortune, who has specialized in the area of clergy abuse, agrees with the concept of a spectrum of clergy offenders. She sees it on a continuum from "wanderers" to "sexual predators." Wanderers are fairly naive and cross boundaries, perhaps ignorant of the damage they've done. Predators are sociopathic and lack conscience.[10]

She also lists traits of all sexual abusers in ministry that appear somewhere on the continuum: controlling, dominating, limited self-awareness, limited or no awareness of boundary issues, no sense of damage caused by their own behavior, poor judgment, limited impulse control, limited understanding of consequences of their actions, often charismatic, sensitive, talented, inspirational and effective in ministry, limited or no awareness of their own power, lack of recognition of their own sexual feelings, confusion of sex and affection.

Building on the work of Schoener and Gonsiorek, Dr. Richard Irons has formulated an archetypal categorization of sexual offenders. Regarding clergy, he describes the following categories:

1. The Naive Prince. This clergy person is usually psychologically healthy but is not trained well enough to perceive boundaries. He or she may be new to ministry and feel invulnerable with the power of status. Given the right circumstances and stress level, this person can become romantically and sexually involved a bit naively.

2. The Wounded Warrior. The church becomes this type of person's professional identity. This pastor usually becomes immersed in a demanding ministry and neglects self-care. Serving others is the main source of self-worth. Shame is a central issue for this person, so he or she receives validation from the outside, including that which is sexual. Repressed wounds from the past fuel current conflicts. This pastor becomes increasingly isolated, and addictions may be present.

3. The Self-Serving Martyr. The clergy person in this category usually is in his or her middle or late career. This person has devoted his or her life to serving the church, sacrificing personal growth and family. Despite this pastor's need to be "the ultimate caregiver," this type eventually resents the congregation's demands. He or she feels unappreciated and abandoned. Anger and resentment lead this person to feelings of entitlement, which leads him or her across sexual boundaries into misconduct.

A long-suffering martyr may become narcissistic and start believing he or she has a special ministry created by God. This person thus believes that no one else fully understands him or her. A type such as this experiences significant anxiety, with the possibility of a variety of addictions, including sexual addiction. He or she may become obsessive-compulsive, narcissistic, dependent, or hysterical.

4. The False Lover. A person in this category displays intensity and high drama. This person loves taking risks, including the thrill of seducing another. He or she may be charming, creative, and energetic, and often creates the impression that he or she is the best minister to ever serve the congregation. The false lover may maintain a series of lovers. He or she may experience divorces, job changes, and other social, legal, and vocational vacillation.

5. The Dark King. This clergy person is best described as charming and charismatic, exploiting his or her power for personal gain. He or she needs to control and can usually find a vulnerable adult for sexual involvement. This type usually has devoted followers who remain loyal despite exposed sexual misconduct. A dark king will go to great lengths to defend himself or herself and can do so convincingly. This type is rare and is usually the one we find in media portrayals.

6. The Wild Card. This person has a major mental disorder. The wild card may seek to manage his or her illness with sexual activity, but not through a pattern or ritual. He or she may appear religious and may have a genuine spirituality.[11]

Assessment theories are usually based on an understanding of male offenders, since most offenders are male. And offenses by women are not perceived as negatively by males.

Women in all denominations can assume positions of power and authority even if they are not fully ordained. We live in a cultural climate where women are taught to be more sexually assertive. We have personally found that women in positions of power in any church can be vulnerable to sexually abusing parishioners, but in smaller numbers than men.

It is fairly rare to see a person at the severe end of the spectrum ("the dark king," sociopathic disorder person). It is far more common to see offenders who are naive, young, uneducated, or inexperienced. It is also far more common to find offenders in the midrange of the spectrum with various personality and emotional factors.

We have gone through this detail about sexual sin, addiction, and abuse because distinctions are important. Accurate assessment of what we are dealing with will help us know what to do. All of us in churches must reach new levels of understanding about these behaviors.

The Bible contains stories of sexual sin and abuse. These have been challenges since the beginning of time. Paul often uses sexual immorality as an indicator of rebellion against God.

In the next two chapters we will look at what makes pastors and others vulnerable to sexual sin, misconduct, addiction, and even committing sexual abuse.

2

Pastoral Vulnerability

Most of us grow up in families. In these family systems, we are all connected and influence each other whether we realize it or not.

Few of us are objective about our families of origin. Therapists often hear those they're counseling say, "I had a perfect childhood." All families do many good things. But all families also make some mistakes. Unfortunately, denial and rationalization are alive and well for even most pastors when they talk about the strengths and weaknesses of the families from which they came. Like anyone else, pastors may bring factors from childhood into their careers. These may become the seeds of sexual sin. Unfortunately, such seeds in the lives of pastors can find plenty of water and fertilizer!

The combination of birth, family, childhood trauma, and pastoral challenges may leave a mammoth vulnerability in the earthen vessel—the pastor. All of us are susceptible to such a fall. Frequently, the pastor who is most certain that he or she would never transgress God's will discovers that such thinking is a seductive trap.

Understanding and dealing with our family systems helps us clarify our identities. Our families give us the basic ways through which we all become a part of society and learn to interact. As we examine our families, we'll see the family values, assumptions, and stereotypes we come from.

A look at your lineage, or the legacy of your family heritage, has biblical precedent. For instance, think of how important the concept of receiving a "blessing" from the father is in the Old Testament (see Gen. 27, Heb. 11:20).

It may be helpful for you to draw a diagram, which most therapists call a genogram, of your family. In order to draw this "map" you will need some symbols. You can use symbols of your choosing, but the following have become universal among counselors and therapists. You will notice that boxes symbolize men and cir-

cles indicate women. Horizontal lines represent marriage, and
vertical lines represent children. A horizontal line with a double
slash means there has been a divorce. You can go back as many
generations as you have space and memory to do. This is simply a
way of "seeing" your family system.

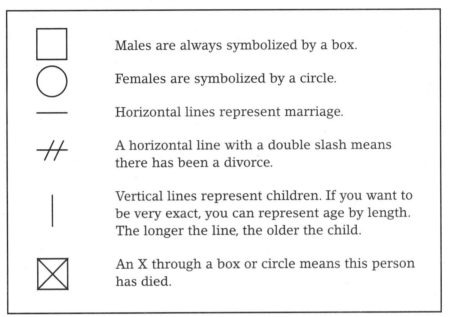

□	Males are always symbolized by a box.
○	Females are symbolized by a circle.
—	Horizontal lines represent marriage.
⫫	A horizontal line with a double slash means there has been a divorce.
|	Vertical lines represent children. If you want to be very exact, you can represent age by length. The longer the line, the older the child.
⊠	An X through a box or circle means this person has died.

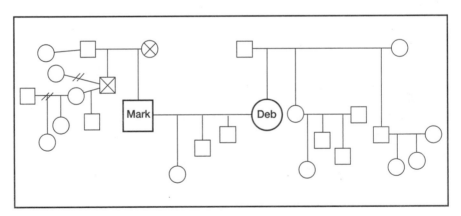

As an example, I have drawn the map of my family. The symbols at the top left represent my father and mother. My mother is
deceased. My father is remarried. My younger brother is represented by the shorter vertical line extending down from the hori-

zontal line that connects my parents. By the diagram you can see my brother was divorced once. His second wife was also divorced and had two daughters from her previous marriage. My brother and his second wife also had one son from their marriage. My brother is now deceased.

My wife, Deb's, parents are represented by the symbols at the top right. Deb has a twin sister and an older brother. You will notice that they each are married and have children.

In the middle of the diagram, you will see that Deb and I have three children: Sarah, our oldest; Jonathan, our middle child; and Benjamin, our youngest.

There are several keys to understanding family dynamics. Let's list five:

1. Boundaries. Every system needs to be safe. Boundaries define safety. Certain behaviors are healthy, and others are not. A safe family does not allow harmful behaviors into the family, but encourages healthy ones. When harmful things happen, boundaries are too loose. When healthy things do not happen, boundaries are too rigid. Boundaries should be like a fence that has some flexibility. Good things get in, and bad things are kept out. When the boundaries are too loose, chaos reigns.

People from families in which loose boundaries are the norm will long for more structure in their lives. In families where rigid boundaries are the norm, the children long for freedom. That is why some people who grow up in "rigid Christian homes" are more vulnerable to addictions, including sexual addiction.[1]

2. Communication. Families should model how to talk honestly about feelings. Some families don't talk and don't accept that deeper emotions even exist. Christians can be guilty of this because they might assume "negative" emotions, such as anger, sadness, or fear, indicate a lack of faith. We might also assume that grown-ups don't cry.

3. Responsibility/Accountability. Mature people accept and confess their mistakes and shortcomings. Immature people seek to deny problems, minimize mistakes, and blame others. Effective role modeling in a family involves admitting problems, saying "I'm sorry," and trying to make amends for damage done.

4. Roles. Many family therapists define roles that family members play. Families have heroes and scapegoats, people who get all the work done (doers), people who crack jokes when the tension gets high (mascots), performers, saints, people who make excuses for others (enablers), and members who get "lost" by seeming so independent they don't need help. Many of us play a variety of roles.

A typical clergy list would be that of hero, saint, and lost child. In these roles they never have problems. In most church families, we see the pastor and parishioners continuing to play roles they learned as children.

> **Unfortunately, in both lay and clergy families sexuality is most often not discussed— good or bad.**

5. Coping Strategies. All families have tension and display ways of coping with it. Alcohol, sports, excessive religious activities, smoking, and drinking caffeine are a few ways families cope. Actually, family members may be very lonely and seeking to medicate the feeling. Substances or behaviors used to cope can become addictive.

All of us as parents and/or grandparents wish that only the best qualities of our families would be passed to further generations. Certainly sexual issues are a fundamental aspect of life inside families. Unfortunately, in both lay and clergy families sexuality is most often not discussed—good or bad. Physical proximity, touch, and exchange of affection are major channels through which families can relate to each other and establish the foundation of healthy sexuality. Each family needs to convey information about healthy sex roles and boundaries. Members of the sexually healthy family respectfully appreciate bodily functions and healthy touch. A healthy Christian family discusses sexual issues openly, communicating about sex in language that is appropriate, reflects morals and attitudes, and helps decision making and problem solving regarding sexual issues.[2]

Sexual ignorance is not bliss. Healthy information needs to be communicated. Talking about sex is not an easy thing. In our culture the blending of two people in marriage transforms the intimate world of their two families into a new family. This is not always a smooth transition. Most of the time we don't examine the effect of our early life experiences until something traumatic occurs. People in the church bring their "baggage" about sex and other issues to their partners.

Family dynamics can offer challenges for anyone, including

pastors. Addictions (work, sex, eating, gambling, religion, and alcohol), domestic violence, emotional cruelty, incest, child abuse, and dysfunctional marriages are some challenges facing clergy families. Let's look at some of the family-of-origin situations that become seeds for disaster.

Jim grew up in a family that always attended church. They seldom missed Sunday School, morning worship, youth group, Sunday evening service, or Wednesday night prayer meeting. They also attended revival services. Jim's dad was on the church board, and his mom taught Sunday School. Both sang in the choir. One night when Jim was 14, he could not sleep well and decided to watch TV. He entered the family room and caught his dad looking at a pornographic magazine and masturbating. His dad had not heard Jim and also was shocked. His dad told him that was the first time he had ever looked at such a magazine and asked Jim not to tell anyone in the family.

Jim kept that promise. However, he then purchased his own magazine and began a pattern of using pornography to fantasize and masturbate. He would stop for several days, but then fall back into the chronic pattern. By the time he was 16, he was masturbating up to three or four times a day. This pattern continued into college. Jim went to a church-related college and felt he could not talk to his professors or a counselor at school. He said he never heard anyone address the issue and believed he would be kicked out of school. His masturbation continued into seminary. When he got married, he thought the chronic masturbation would end. However, he discovered he was masturbating at least two or three times a day. When he tried to masturbate less, he found he couldn't quit. He said his daily ritual was the most exciting part of his day. When his wife discovered his stash of pornography, she insisted that he get professional help.

Family systems theory helps us understand families in distress because of pornography. The pastor who grows up in a chaotic family may feel a need to latch on to something for security. This provides the basis for vulnerability. The rigid family provides the possibility of reacting with rebellion and lack of control.

Since the family is the primary context of human experience, a significant study of pastoral vulnerability mandates looking closely at the pastor's family. Transgenerational views of the family, the "sins of the father being passed down," help to understand the evolution of both problems and solutions across many generations of the family. Frequently, family interactions reflect patterns inherited from ancestors. Therapeutic solutions involve addressing issues in a person's family of origin.

We also believe it is important to look at factors beyond the relational bonds of the family, such as extended family; gender roles defined by culture, religion, politics, and economic norms; and relationships with church members and ecclesiastical authorities.

All families change over time. Every transition—birth, school, marriage, divorce—requires change in the family. When a family has difficulty meeting the challenges of a life-cycle stage or moving to the next stage, a crisis may occur. The pastor needs to understand these challenges in his or her family of origin and present family.

An example of this kind of dynamic for many pastors is that they may be "stuck" (or "arrested") at certain developmental stages of childhood. In short, they have never grown up. This could mean such pastors can't or won't accept the responsibilities of adulthood. Becoming an adult with a personal separate identity is one of the great tasks of development. We often see pastors who are not independent. They may act as if they are, but they are actually needy and dependent. We have seen many congregations in which an immature pastor is leading immature people, and they are all playing out their childhood issues with each other. Have you ever been to a church meeting that seemed more like the junior high lunchroom?

When the pastor is immature, he or she may let some members in the congregation or staff people become the nurturers in an unhealthy way. For example, Paul was a pastor who was still heavily nurtured by his mom and was frustrated that his wife did not nurture him as much. He had a sensitive, attractive secretary who pampered him as his mother did, and built his ego. He began to spend more time with his secretary. They would sometimes hug each other. Before long, the hugging evolved into fondling. Fortunately the secretary felt guilty and quit her job. His guilt led him to disclose this and his pornography use to his wife.

These disclosures partially resulted from his attending a denominational seminar about sexual boundaries. His double life scared him, and he confessed and asked for forgiveness from God and his wife. This was a huge wake-up call. His wife insisted that they get professional help to understand how he had started such behavior. They clearly knew they loved each other, and both wanted their relationship to improve rather than end.

They began to explore their lives and family histories individually and together in therapy.

Some aspects of Paul's family of origin helped him understand his double life. Paul was a third generation minister who had known stoic paternal grandparents. His dad was a pastor who did not express feelings. His mother pampered him and appeared to try to make up for his father's coldness to him. Paul remembered feeling uncomfortable as a child with both of his parents' modes of relating to him. He had two sisters who were affectionate toward him, so he experienced enormous nurturing from the females in his house. At times he felt smothered by the warmth and enjoyed his dad's aloofness. Soon after he married Joan, he realized she seldom showed affection, and she was jealous of his attention from his family. They became distant from his family. Paul had learned from his father how to internalize his feelings. He became lonely for his family and began to resent Joan.

He also never shared with Joan that he had occasionally masturbated with pornography from early adolescence. The combination of masturbation and pornography became a very powerful drug in Paul's life, which continued through college, seminary, and his dating years with Joan. He thought when he got married, his desire to masturbate and look at pornography would decrease or end. But after three or four months of marriage, he was again regularly looking at pornography and masturbating. He had never talked to anyone about this sinful part of his life. He had often asked God to deliver him from the habit.

When the combination of pornography, masturbation, and sexual behaviors with his secretary occurred, he became depressed. Joan and a few others noticed his despair. When his secretary resigned, he felt that he could no longer keep secrets from Joan. All of these aspects were dealt with in therapy.

In her therapy, Joan also was learning much about her background. In her family, neither parent had expressed feelings. Performance was rewarded, so Joan did well academically. She received much validation from church members and from Paul for her ability to play the organ and lead a women's Bible study group. Joan felt good about the couple's leadership. But she felt a tremendous loneliness in her marriage. She didn't know how to express her feelings toward Paul. She would hold in feelings of both love and frustration and try to express her love by doing more things for him.

> **Some messages from childhood, such as "boys don't cry," can impair the adult male.**

In couples therapy they discovered they both wanted more nurturing in the relationship but had never discussed that need. As frequently happens, Paul's inappropriate behavior made the couple realize they had other important challenges in the area of intimacy. Paul learned to communicate his feelings and thus in that area be different from his father. Joan learned the importance of communicating feelings. They discovered they could change their communication styles and not carry on the dysfunctional communication practices of their families.

The role of family members in sexual vulnerability is still poorly understood both by mental health professionals and ministry leaders. Understanding more about the family of origin helps pastors understand their personal issues and helps with their relapse prevention. Pastors who turn to pornography often have family histories of denial, low self-worth, repressed feelings, self-delusions, and the lack of healthy sex education.

Some messages from childhood, such as "boys don't cry," can impair the adult male. This dynamic may be coupled in a marriage with a wife who was taught that girls should always be nice. A common challenge of church families is the understanding that it is inappropriate to talk, think, or feel about sex. Another rule in many pastors' families is to first work and then if play occurs to have it much later. Frequently the older child is expected to set the example for the younger children. Another common family rule is that family members are never to talk about their family outside of the home, because "nothing is worse than being disloyal to your family."

Think about rules that were spoken or wordlessly communicated to you. Some family members try to live up to unworkable rules, which results in failure. As a result, these people face inadequacy, guilt, hurt, abandonment, and anger.

Many pastors have incredible anger or rage because of repressed emotions. Before they can deal with the myriads of issues that people in their congregations face, pastors need to experience repair work in their own lives. When they don't, they often hit bottom, using pornography, and so on, before they begin to change.

Unfortunately, pastors raised in Christ-centered homes have not necessarily received more nurturing and self-esteem messages than those who grew up in unbelieving homes. Affirmations during childhood are essential to childrens' emotional growth. Many pastors feel they never experienced unconditional love in their families but were led to believe they fell short of God's and their parents' wills for their lives. If a pastor grew up in a rigid family with very little understanding of God's grace, he or she will be more likely to break rules.

One possible manifestation of this is to make inappropriate sexual choices. Another frequent challenge in such families is the use of anger in communication. When a pastor grows up in a home where a parent was explosive in temperament, the pastor frequently has challenges dealing with anger in marriage and in the church.

Doice grew up in a home with parents who regularly raged at each other. At about age 12, Doice discovered that masturbation was a way to escape his parents' yelling. Somewhere in his church experience, he heard the message that masturbation was a sin. As a 29-year-old pastor, he felt a great deal of confusion about his sexuality. He wondered whether his masturbation, which his wife didn't know about, was both sexual sin and a type of marital infidelity. His inability to stop masturbating caused growing guilt.

When Doice first discovered Internet pornography, he was like the "kid in the candy store." But this candy store provided such an adrenaline rush that his masturbation habits began to last from half an hour to three hours a day. Ashamed, he would avoid the subject of sexuality with his youth group and congregation. A crisis occurred when Doice's five-year-old walked into the room while he had pornography on the computer screen. His son did not see the screen, but the incident propelled Doice to get some professional help and work on addiction.

With all the pastors we have treated who have crossed inappropriate sexual boundaries, we have found roots of their inappropriate behavior in their families of origin. Some of the pastors had parents who were religious fanatics. We believe there is such a thing as religious addiction. Such a family is obsessed with religion, and an extreme effort to preserve religious values dominates most every family interaction. Such a family differs from an alcoholic family, for instance, only because alcohol is not present. All other patterns run parallel. Members of this kind of family do not talk about emotions.

There is a direct correlation between the lack of self-care and vulnerability to sexual temptation.

Childhood lessons frequently include statements about the self that can be destructive for the pastor, such as these:

• "I cannot depend on people because people are unpredictable."

In many pastors' homes where family members indulged in compulsive behavior, pastors learned that people change from one minute to the next and may be unpredictable or explosive. Therefore, people cannot be depended on.

Darryl, who as an adult followed in his father's footsteps of having compulsive affairs and an obsession with pornography, was always afraid of his father who was a womanizer and had a violent temper. Darryl said he never knew how his father would react. "If I did something wrong, he might explode. If I did something right, he might hit me anyway."

This unpredictability created stress in Darryl that was not alleviated by his profession. Some of the explosive members of his church board created trauma for Darryl partly because of his father's raging. When Darryl discovered one of the people he could not depend on was himself, he began to face the challenge of being both a pastor and a Jekyll-and-Hyde Christian.

• "I am nothing without other people's approval."

Unfortunately what we now call codependency has frequently been encouraged as the Christian way. The scripture 1 Cor. 8:13, "Therefore, if what I eat causes my brother to fall into sin, I will never eat meat again, so that I will not cause him to fall," has been used to support an unhealthy taking care of others at the expense of self-care. There is a direct correlation between the lack of self-care and vulnerability to sexual temptation.

• "If people can't get near me, they can't hurt me."

When a pastor grows up in a home with much physical or emotional aggression, he or she fears intimacy and often chronically uses pornography. Using pornography may feel safer to the pastor than human relationships.

Martha, who was an associate pastor of a large urban congregation, grew up in a home where her father regularly hit and yelled at her and her siblings. She stated, "I always feared being physically hurt. Even as a pastor, I assumed that if I gave people a chance to hurt me, they would."

Martha turned to "soft porn" to escape from the stress of work.

- "I must be perfect. If I make mistakes, tragedy will occur."

Perfectionism has caused enormous pain for many pastors and spouses. "Not being good enough" is a common theme in ministry families. Most pastors who cross sexual boundaries feel insecure about their own abilities. This family pressure is topped by the challenge of the unrealistic expectations congregations put on their ministers.

- "If I say what I really need and think, I will lose love and approval."

Those raised in families with poor communication appear to be at high risk for participating in sexual sin. Too often the church has also discouraged "truth-telling." When parents do not encourage independent thinking in a child, healthy assertiveness is not a learned behavior.

These childhood lessons are just a few examples of the power for good or ill in families. The following questions might help you take an audit of your own family formation.

- Did your parents have severe marital problems? If so, describe the effects of their unhealthy communication on your life.
- Did any secrets in your family create a pattern of deceit in your own life?
- Was spirituality a healthy resource in your family of origin?
- Do you recognize any patterns of addiction in your family?
- Did your parents—through words or actions—teach you how to trust or not trust others?
- Did you have permission to show your feelings as a child?
- What happened when someone expressed feelings in your family?
- Did you receive any formal sex education? If so, did that education positively influence your life?

- How do you hope your family will be similar or different from your family of origin?
- If you have crossed sexual boundaries as an adult, what can you trace to early messages or childhood experiences that negatively influenced your sexual development?
- As a child I was taught to regard sex as _____.
- How did you view your parents' sexuality? Was affection shown openly at home?
- If you grew up in a religious home, did religion enhance your understanding of healthy sexuality? Was masturbation forbidden by your family or your religion?
- Were you ever sexually, physically, or emotionally abused as a child?
- Were you ever caught masturbating? If so, were you punished?
- Did your family have constant chaos that other families did not appear to have?

Church members bring their own family-of-origin issues into congregations. Most pastors realize that church systems are frequently as "crazy" as the families from which they themselves came. So pastors constantly face interactions that can create enormous stress, reminding them of what they have experienced all their lives.

A pastor can rarely look objectively at his family-of-origin issues unless he or she receives that perspective in pastoral training. Too many times, a crisis forces the issue. The stress of these family issues creates a loneliness that creates vulnerability. When vulnerability leads to sexual sin, we face the opportunity to heal. No issue more clearly reminds us that we are truly earthen vessels (2 Cor. 4:7) than sexual infidelity.

In the next chapter we will describe how families can create wounds in a pastor's heart and spirit as we continue to try to understand vulnerability.

3

Wounds

W e are all fragile beings and need to be protected from harm, loved, nurtured, affirmed, and touched in healthy ways. As we have described in chapter 2, some families easily provide those elements. Others don't. A family is never all good or all bad at doing so. Some of our needs weren't met, while some were. When we understand this, we can also begin understanding how we might have been wounded in our families. We don't have to believe our parents are awful and evil people to understand our wounds. Most of our parents were doing the best job they could. They were probably dealing with their own fears, anxieties, loneliness, or ignorance.

If you can surrender any judgment of how bad your family was, you'll better grasp the dynamics of this chapter.

As we discussed in chapter 2 (see p. 24), two kinds of safety issues can occur in families. The first occurs when boundaries are invaded. The second happens when boundaries are so rigid they block healthy love and nurture. Experts in family theory and in addictions divide these differences into two categories of invasion or neglect/abandonment. This can happen in different aspects of a person's life. We might look at it like this:[1]

	Emotional	Physical	Sexual	Spiritual
Invasion				
Neglect/ Abandonment				

FIGURE 1

This diagram provides a way to categorize wounds that can have lasting effects. It helps us understand that these categories overlap in their ability to affect each other. Here is a brief description of each:

"Emotional invasion" occurs when we are led to believe we are bad and worthless people. This can be the result of put-downs, criticism, name-calling, shouting, teasing, comparisons, unhealthy anger, and more. Sometimes these forms of invasion can be dramatic, such as parents who say, "You are really stupid!" Sometimes people are even told they are mistakes.

One pastor's mother was 42 years old when he was born. He was an "accident" in that he was not planned. Every day of his young life his mother told him "I regret the day you were born" in some way or another.

At other times these forms of invasion are mentioned casually, such as, "I'm not surprised you couldn't do that right; you've never been very good at those kinds of things." Often we are compared, "You're older brother could do that." Sometimes we are teased, but the words cut to the core of our soul

The message that something is wrong with us is not always verbal. Some of us have received "the look that could kill," the pointed finger, or "the sigh." Our parents or others didn't directly express displeasure but still communicated it. Since they don't really express what they are feeling, we interpret that something must be wrong with us or this wouldn't be happening.

We can be emotionally invaded as children if our feelings are not validated. Some call this mind rape. We might be sad, frightened, or angry. Someone might have talked us out of our reality by saying, "That's a stupid thing to feel" or "Big boys don't cry" or "Don't be scared. Be a man."

If we grew up in a Christian home, this message might even be expressed, "God doesn't like it when you feel that way."

When caregivers around us, such as our parents and teachers, are lonely, they may turn to us for emotional support. We become their confidants. We may like being considered so "adult." When one of our parents is doing this, we become like a surrogate spouse. Even at ages two, three, and four we can be turned into "adult" companions for lonely parents and caregivers. They may even affirm us by saying, "You're my special buddy, and I don't know what I'd do without you. You make me so proud."

This dynamic is often been referred to as "emotional incest."[2] Pastors have often been raised in this kind of relationship and learn how to care for adults at early ages. They have never known how to be a child because they took on the responsibility of caring for others.

Emotional invasion impairs our positive sense of self. We think we are not worthy, that something must be wrong with us. We lose the ability to affirm and care for ourselves and think our only worth is in performance (that is never perfect enough) or by taking care of others. "Shame" is the word that often describes the constellation of feelings with this negative sense of self.

> **Emotional invasion impairs our positive sense of self.**

Shame is not inherently negative. It can remind us that we are imperfect and need each other and God. When shame becomes unhealthy, it tells us we don't deserve God's love and acceptance. What is the distinction between guilt and shame? Guilt is the knowledge we've made a mistake. Shame is the feeling we *are* a mistake.

"Emotional abandonment" is the flip side of invasion and in many ways more powerfully produces shame. We all need a certain amount of affirmation and attention. We need to be listened to. Others who are older, wiser, and more mature need to listen to us when we are small and help us figure out what we're feeling. We need to be affirmed for stating our feelings, even if we do so imperfectly. We need to be praised just for who we are, not because someone wants something from us or because we have performed according to someone else's agenda.

Many of us didn't get this positive nurturing. And it's hard to understand because we didn't even know we weren't getting it. In this experience, we grow up lonely but don't even know we're lonely. We feel shame but don't know we do. We have feelings but don't recognize them because no one helped us to have them. Later in life we get into relationships and find people accusing us of not feeling, and we have no idea what they're talking about.

"Physical invasion" occurs when a child is hit, slapped, or even spanked in anger. Many of the people we deal with were excessively beaten with their fathers' belts. One of our pastor friends says, "It's as if my dad thought my brains were in my backside and, if it was stimulated enough, I would get smarter." Physical invasion can leave lasting wounds of fear.

Some of us grew up in homes where others were abused. Even if we only saw it, the effect can be the same. We learned about this when Vietnam veterans came home. They lived in a violent time and in a violent culture, fighting a "conflict" with no front lines. They were in danger wherever they were. Many of these men and women suffered posttraumatic stress disorder even though they weren't in combat. Similarly, many who were only observers still experience a degree of ongoing trauma following the savage attack on September 11, 2001, in New York and Washington, D.C. This sort of trauma also happens in a violent home.

"Physical abandonment" can mean our basic needs weren't met, such as food, clothing, and shelter. It might mean we were often left alone. Most powerfully, it can be that we weren't touched enough in healthy ways. We all know newborn babies need to be held often. If they aren't, they fail to thrive and can possibly even die. Many of the people we deal with are "touch deprived." They, too, fail to thrive.

Many sexual activities are as much an attempt to be touched as to have a full sexual experience. One pastor told us that every time he went to a prostitute, he simply wanted to be held and touched.

"Sexual invasion" has been more fully understood in the last 25 years. It includes being molested or raped—penetrated sexually by the use of some kind of power—physically, emotionally, or spiritually. Many people were sexually abused without considering it as such. Being sexual with an older teenager, for example, may have been considered sexual experimentation. For something to be abusive, remember, it needs to leave an emotional and spiritual wound. Some young people were sexual with an adult and considered it a "right of passage." Teenage boys sometimes view being sexual with an older woman in this way. What is important are the lasting effects this experience may have had.

Being exposed to pornography at early ages can start a lifetime pattern.

Sexual humor and teasing can damage us. Being teased about the size, shape, or attractiveness of our bodies can hurt. Comments about gender, physical development (such as menstruation), and personal characteristics (such as being male and seeming a bit feminine) can leave lasting scars.

We also shouldn't forget the abusive effects culture can have. Being exposed to pornography at early ages, for example, can start a lifetime pattern. We hear countless stories about people finding a parent's "stash" of material. Stories and jokes we tell each other, many of them sexual myths, can stay in our minds.

We wonder how many people realize we are being sexually invaded by culture. If you turn on your TV, for example, you will be exposed to sexual images you didn't invite into your life. If you stand in the checkout lane of a grocery store and look at the covers of magazines, you will see images that would have been the centerfold of magazines 40 years ago. Go into an average hotel room these days, and if you press certain buttons, you will see graphic pornography. Finally, remember how many E-mails you get that are sexual in nature or how many times you may have stumbled across a sexual web site.

"Sexual abandonment" primarily means that we haven't received information and modeling of healthy sexuality. Can you remember information about sexuality that was given to you when you were young? Where did it come from? Did you receive it at home, at school, or at church? Perhaps you heard basic biological information years after you already knew. Most of us have stories of how embarrassing it was for our parents to talk to us about sex.

We have talked to countless Christians who don't remember helpful information coming from church. Many remember the scare tactics about sexual sin usually using words such as "perversion" and "fornication." No one talked about healthy sexuality or positive reasons for abstinence before marriage and faithfulness in marriage. Sex became a scary subject, and most of us probably became all the more curious about the "secret" nature of it.

One way physical and sexual dimensions overlap is through the absence of healthy physical touch. We all need a certain amount of physical touch in our lives. Our parents and caregivers are responsible to touch us in healthy ways. When we don't receive that enough, it impairs us. Often people will substitute sexual touch for the healthy touching they really need. In families who have an absence of affirming physical touch, children may pursue misguided sexual avenues.

So where did we learn about sex? We were left to hear about it from our friends or glean what we could from music, TV, movies, advertising, and magazines, such as the pornographic kind. We talk to many people who are educated about sex through the question-and-answer columnists in magazines. If you look at some of these forums in magazines, you will see how many myths about sex and morality they portray.

It is more difficult to define what can be considered a "spiritual invasion." Various theological viewpoints exist on appropriate communication to children about God and religious practices. When religion is talked about only negatively, this can have a damaging effect on people.

Mark Laaser tells a story about a Bible study he and his wife attended. The host couple had a three-year-old daughter who was trying to play by herself and not interrupt her parents. When she fell down the stairs while trying to slide down the banister and bumped her head, the mother said, "I wonder if Jesus wanted you playing on the banister? If He had, He wouldn't have let you bump your head." This kind of teaching sets up a fear-based image of Jesus.

Religion can also be invasive when we are talked out of our feelings for religious reasons. We may have heard statements such as, "It's not Christlike to feel that way" or "Would God like those thoughts?" We are left to believe that Christians are always happy and at peace. If we have any thoughts and feelings that aren't positive, we feel we aren't trusting God and His providence. This kind of theology leaves no room for problems, anger, or depression. Many of the main characters in the Bible seem to struggle with these feelings. We Christians, however, expect a different standard of ourselves.

At times, the correct theology is delivered to us at difficult times, causing us to deny our true feelings. Fifteen years ago Mark Laaser was sobbing at his grandmother's funeral. The kind pastor put his arm around him and said, "I would remind you of your faith. You will see your grandmother again. Smile and reflect the joy you have in salvation."

After that kind of statement, you don't know whether to say, "Amen" or "I know I'll see my grandmother again, but is it OK to be sad today?"

One powerful way to recognize spiritual invasion is to remember that if any of the other forms of invasion or abandonment happen and the person responsible represents religion or God to us, the effect is spiritual. If a minister, for example, is sexual with a parishioner, very significant spiritual damage occurs. If a father or mother is a pillar of a church or is very religious, nearly anything this parent does can have very powerful spiritual effect.

As therapists, we work with many people that are spiritually damaged. They have a very hard time trusting a loving and graceful God. They may not be able to imagine God as a loving and gentle Father. They may think His grace is for everyone else but them. We work with lots of pastors who preach about a loving God but don't accept that He loves them.

Many of the same things can be said about spiritual abandonment. All of us should ask who our positive role models were regarding faith. It is not a matter of whether or not our parents or caregivers took us to church or had devotions at home. Did they practice what they preached? Did they demonstrate in their daily actions what they believed? Did they reflect healthy characteristics of God, or did they seem like hypocrites?

> **Ask God to show you any wounds in your heart and soul that still need healing.**

Even though many of us were raised in the church and submitted to much religious discipline, we may never have seen a relationship with Christ truly lived out. We might wonder what the value is of such a relationship if it doesn't affect the way a person acts.

At this point, we would ask you to pray a simple prayer, asking God to show you any wounds in your heart and soul that still need healing. As you read about the issues we raised and the stories we told, what memories came to you? We believe the Holy Spirit may talk to us even through memories. You may still be experiencing places of deep pain, anger, sadness, and grieving. These feelings and memories can definitely affect how you react to life today. Today, at times someone will say or do something that takes you back to the time you were first wounded. Have you ever, for example, felt that your sadness or anger was an overreaction to a current situation? Has anyone ever asked you, "Why are you getting so upset about such a minor thing?"

We all get "triggered" into feelings and memories. We may not be aware of how they are affecting us. We can only learn healthy reactions to these realities when we know they can occur. We can, in other words, learn how to control our reactions. We can't control the fact that we will have reactions.

We have prepared a "thorn in the flesh" inventory. It is a simply list of yes-or-no questions that might help you assess where your vulnerabilities are. This is not to be considered as a psychological test or as a predictor that you will automatically have problems.

"THORN IN THE FLESH" INVENTORY

1. Did you grow up in a family with boundary problems?
2. Did you grow up in a family that didn't openly express feelings?
3. In your family, did people get angry about the wrong religious answers?
4. Was sexual abuse present in any form in your family?
5. Did your family practice any physical abuse?
6. Did you grow up in a family without affirmations?
7. Did you or anyone consider your family perfect?
8. Did either of your parents seem angry, lonely, sick, or tired?
9. Did either of your parents expect you to take care of them?
10. Were addictions such as alcoholism, work, sex, food, or spending present in your family?
11. Were either of your parents frequently absent from your home?
12. Did you grow up with healthy sex education?
13. Was any pornography or explicit sexual activity in your home?
14. When you were growing up, did you feel that no one understood you?
15. Do you feel that the members of your congregation treat you poorly?
16. Do you feel that your spouse doesn't understand you?
17. Did your seminary training prepare you for self-care?
18. At times do you think that God doesn't care about you or answer your prayers?
19. Do you frequently think that you are in the wrong profession?

20. Do you frequently feel depressed or lonely but are afraid to admit it?

21. Do you often feel angry and resentful?

22. Do you find it impossible to participate in fellowship for yourself?

23. Do you think you have lots of acquaintances but no true friends?

24. Do you resist being accountable to others?

25. Do you sometimes believe you lead a double life?

26. Do you think that no one understands you?

27. Do you have a great deal of marital stress?

28. Do you frequently experience sexual frustration?

29. Do you frequently feel bored?

30. Do you believe the only reason people like you is because of your role?

31. Do you take on everyone else's pain and sorrow without taking care of your own, or do you take care of everyone else and not yourself?

This may help you see your own vulnerability. If you find that you have answered yes to a number of the above questions, you may want to discuss them with a counselor who may be able to assess your situation more deliberately and accurately.

In the next chapter we will begin discussing what healthy sexuality is. We hope and pray that this begins a journey of self-awareness for you that will lead to a more healthy and fulfilling life.

4

Healthy Sexuality

W e have tried in the first three chapters of this book to present how pastors and others become vulnerable to sexual sin and temptation. Unhealed wounds from the past can cause us to be lonely and angry. Loneliness and anger combined with a normal sex drive can create the false belief that sex is the answer to all of our needs for touch, affirmation, and nurture.

Books like this would be totally depressing if we didn't spend more time outlining healing and the hope to be sexually whole. We believe that Christians must understand and strive for healthy sexuality. So many of us are hungering for *positive* reasons to achieve sexual wholeness. Young people today want to know why they should wait until marriage to have sex. They tell us they know what God wants them not to do, but they wonder why.

We can't remain silent about these issues. We must discuss them. We believe there are many positive reasons why God intends for sex to only be expressed in marriage. What are they?

At the end of this chapter we will outline a model that can help build sexual wholeness. The model contains five dimensions. In each of the next chapters we will describe the meaning and challenges of those dimensions. In this chapter we begin by trying to understand a biblical basis for healthy sexuality. We pray that the rest of this book will stimulate your own thoughts and prayers and personal answers to this great challenge.

Any person will be disappointed if he or she thinks maintaining sexual fidelity or sobriety depends on achieving biological sexual satisfaction. Having sex in marriage that is both enjoyable and fulfilling depends on so much more than the biological mechanics of sex. We believe that God intended it that way. We believe too much emphasis has been placed on the physical act of sex. Our culture seems to teach us that mind-blowing sex for a lifetime is the "Holy Grail" we all should seek. If we watch any TV, listen to any popular music, look at any magazine rack, or see any movies, we will be tempted to think that the whole world is either having sex or figuring out ways to have it better. Take a moment and note how many sexual messages have bombarded you today. Before we can understand the biblical view of sexual health, we need to understand the level of intimacy that can exist between a husband and wife.

In the Old Testament, we find some cornerstone biblical truths about sexuality. After relaying the creation of the first man and woman, Adam and Eve, the Bible says, "For this reason a man will leave his father and mother and be united to his wife, and they will become one flesh. The man and his wife were both naked, and they felt no shame" (Gen. 2:24-25). Man and woman were created for each other, to help each other. According to the Bible, Adam and Eve sinned because of their own unwillingness to trust and obey God. They were selfish enough to disobey God. Something about selfishness and pride is a vital aspect of our search for truth about sexuality.

When we start with the idea that something is so sacred in the union of a man and woman that it is called a "one-flesh union," we are on the right track. We should then remember the teaching of the Ten Commandments. We are to be sexually faithful in marriage. We are not to commit adultery, and we are not to covet another's spouse.

This is a tall order as we live in a sexually saturated culture and deal with our own natural biological desires. We believe something about spiritual attitude and spiritual intimacy between a husband and wife makes honoring these commandments possible. Understanding what that spiritual attitude and that spiritual intimacy are will be critical to remaining faithful.

A word search for "sex" in the Bible is a frustrating experience. The word "sex" is only used twice in the NIV (Gen. 19:4, Judg. 19:22). Both times that it is used, it refers to the intent by "wicked men" to have sex with other men. The Bible is clear, however, about the evils of certain forms of sexual immorality. The seventh commandment (Exod. 20:14), about not committing adultery, receives the most attention. Jesus' teaching on this commandment, in Matt 5:28, is frightening for all those of us who have ever fantasized. Jesus says, "But I tell you that anyone who looks at a woman lustfully has already committed adultery with her in his heart."

In this teaching Jesus seems to tell us that our thought life is more important than our actions. He is speaking to all self-righteous people who might say, "I never actually had sex with that person." Our attitude about what we long for and what we are thinking is an important spiritual issue to consider.

The word "prostitute" appears more than 50 times in the Bible. We read repeated warnings about the dangers of getting involved with "harlots." Paul goes so far as to say that a man who "unites" with a prostitute becomes one flesh with her (see 1 Cor. 6:16). James uses the prostitute Rahab (as described in Josh. 2) as an example that even she, a prostitute, is righteous because of her good deeds (see James 2:25). In the story of the prodigal son (Luke 15), the older brother accuses the prodigal of squandering all of his money with prostitutes (v. 30).

The word "lust" appears in the Bible 13 times and is generally associated with evil desires and idolatry. In Col. 3:5, Paul says, "Put to death, therefore, whatever belongs to your earthly nature: sexual immorality, impurity, lust, evil desires and greed, which is idolatry." The English word "lust" is taken from the German word that can be positively used to refer to anything that is desired. The Bible is more emphatic that lust can pertain to a desire for anything that is forbidden. This implies that lust refers to any selfish desire. We are urged to purge ourselves of selfish desire.

Paul teaches the Galatians, "Those who belong to Christ Jesus have crucified the sinful nature with its passions and desires (Gal. 5:24). In his first letter, John exhorts us, "For everything in the world—the cravings of sinful man, the lust of his eyes and the boasting of what he has and does—comes not from the Father but from the world. The world and its desires pass away, but the man who does the will of God lives forever" (1 John 2:16-17).

References to adulterous women are also used to teach about lust. In Prov. 6:25-26 we are instructed, "Do not lust in your heart after her beauty or let her captivate you with her eyes, for the prostitute reduces you to a loaf of bread, and the adulteress preys upon your very life."

We find ourselves longing for more specific instruction on sexual practices. One frequently asked question, for example, is about whether masturbation is sinful. The word never appears in the Bible. Many Christians have therefore assumed it should be included in the category of unnatural sexual acts. We also recognize that many sex therapists, including some Christian counselors, use fantasy and masturbation as a therapeutic tool to help couples heal from sexual dysfunctions. We believe too many Christians get stuck arguing about sexual practices such as masturbation when it would be more helpful to understand whether or not the fantasies being used are healthy for that individual. (We will have more to say about unhealthy fantasies in chapters 5 and 7.)

> **This strong man was vulnerable to his own desires.**

Some of the stories in the Bible that involve sex can help us understand biblical principles about healthy sexuality. In the story of Samson we read, "One day Samson went to Gaza, where he saw a prostitute. He went in to spend the night with her" (Judg. 16:1).

The Philistines knew he had been with a prostitute because they had tried to trap him while he was with her. Immediately after this story we read that Samson fell in love with Delilah. The Philistines used Delilah to bring down Samson. This story clearly illustrates that if we pursue our selfish and perhaps dependent sexual and romantic desires, we will lose all of our strength. We may accept that Samson, God's strongest man, was lonely and stressed in his leadership role. Even this strong man was vulnerable to his own desires.

We know of King David's adultery with Bathsheba and his arrangement to have her husband, Uriah, killed. Let's note one of the events leading to that. When David brought the ark of the covenant into Jerusalem, a great and rather rowdy celebration began. David danced around the ark in some state of undress. David's wife, Michal, Saul's daughter, said when he returned home, "How the king of Israel has distinguished himself today, disrobing in the sight of the slave girls of his servants as any vulgar fellow would!" (2 Sam 6:20). The Bible adds this postscript to the story: "And Michal daughter of Saul had no children to the day of her death" (v. 23).

In this context, later, "David got up from his bed and walked around on the roof of the palace. From the roof he saw a woman bathing. The woman was very beautiful" (11:2). Perhaps if the Internet had been available to David, he might have been tempted to get involved in Internet sexual fulfillment. He was probably a lonely leader and possibly living in an unfulfilling marriage. Perhaps the Bible is teaching us that loneliness leads to sexual vulnerability.

First Kings 11 tells us that David's son, Solomon, "loved many foreign women" and they turned him to other gods. Nehemiah 13 describes how these foreign women turned Solomon's heart away from God, just as foreign women had turned away his father, David. Solomon was quite poetic with his love. As we know, the Song of Songs has been used by many as a great love poem that is quite sexually erotic in nature. Loving many women can totally distract us from God.

This lineage of David, the family system he created, is passed on to the next generation in two other sons, Amnon and Absalom. In 2 Sam. 13 is the horrible story of how Amnon molested his sister Tamar and then cast her out of his house. Absalom came to his sister's aid but didn't even let her talk about it, saying, "Don't take this thing to heart." She lived in his house a "desolate woman" (v. 20).

This story teaches us about the power of sexual abuse. Like so many stories, it displays how selfish lust destroys a life and how silence about our pain can be a prison.

The Bible, as we've said, is very harsh about adultery. It is no surprise, then, that the New Testament shows two examples of God's grace demonstrated through the stories of two adulterous women. In John 4 we read of a woman of Samaria who had been married five times and was living with another man.

In Jesus' day, this was about as bad as it could get. She was a Samaritan, a woman, and an adulterer. She went to a well at a time of the day when no one else would be there. However, Jesus talked to this woman and taught her about salvation. Jesus never went into her town to preach—but this woman returns to Samaria. Her shame was relieved, and she proclaimed the good news of what she received from Jesus.

John 8 tells us the story of the woman caught in adultery. In those days, the punishment for adultery was to be stoned. The Bible tells us the teachers of the law and the Pharisees were trying to trap Jesus into arguing about the Law by bringing this woman to Him to see what He would say should be done with her. Jesus avoided the question by simply saying that anyone who was without sin could cast the first stone. When everyone left, He instructed the woman to go and lead a sinless life.

These stories are comforting to any of us who have sexually sinned. They are powerful examples of the true nature of God's grace. Perhaps the greatest example of God's forgiveness is the story of the prodigal son. This story teaches us the relationship between selfishness, rebellion, and sexual sin.

The prodigal son rebelled against his father. In those days you didn't ask for your inheritance while your father was still alive. So this son was really saying that he wished his father were dead. It was an act of total rebellion and selfishness. It led to all the foolishness of wasting the money in a foreign land. We imagine that some money was also spent on wine, food, and other material things.

> **The Bible often uses sexuality to teach us about self-centered desire.**

The Bible often uses sexuality to teach us about self-centered desire. It is not surprising that sexual immorality shows up in teachings about selflessness. Eph. 5, for example, opens with these words, "Be imitators of God, therefore, as dearly loved children and live a life of love, just as Christ loved us and gave himself up for us as a fragrant offering and sacrifice to God. But among you there must not be even a hint of sexual immorality, or of any kind of impurity, or of greed, because these are improper for God's holy people" (vv. 1-3).

In this passage, Paul teaches us about the attitude of humility and selflessness we need to avoid sexual immorality. We must be willing to lead a life of sacrifice, just as Christ loved the Church. Christ died for the Church. We must be willing to die to our selfish desires in order to be sexually pure. This might even be what Paul intends in his teaching in Rom. 12:2, "Do not conform any longer to the pattern of this world, but be transformed by the renewing of your mind."

At the end of the Eph. 5, Paul returned to this theme after teaching about husbands and wives in the middle of the chapter. He says that as he has been describing the one-flesh union of a man and woman in marriage, he was "talking about Christ and the church" (v. 32). In his description of how a husband and wife submit to each other, submission means selflessness and sacrifice. It is not an act to be abused by one spouse. Both husband and wife are to be selfless.

This means sex should never be expressed selfishly, even in

marriage. All those who have done marriage counseling know what selfish sexuality can do to a marriage. The sexually selfish can even abuse Bible passages for their own means. Paul's teaching about wives' submission in Eph. 5:22-24 is one such passage. Another teaching appears in 1 Cor. 7: 4 when Paul writes, "The wife's body does not belong to her alone but also to her husband. In the same way, the husband's body does not belong to him alone but also to his wife."

We believe that Paul was referring to an attitude of selflessness and not about specific sexual responsibilities. This attitude is to be mutual. Often in marriages, unfortunately, passages such as these are used by one spouse to manipulate the other.

If the husband and wife's relationship is like that of Christ and the Church, the love between them must be the highest form of love. It is a selfless and sacrificial love. In Paul's famous teaching on love in 1 Cor. 13, he describes love this way: "Love is patient, love is kind. It does not envy, it does not boast, it is not proud. It is not rude, it is not self-seeking, it is not easily angered, it keeps no record of wrongs" (vv. 4-5). This is a selfless love.

If we put two biblical truths about sexuality together, we will understand that the biblical view of healthy sexuality is to be expressed in the sacred covenant of monogamous marriage and that marital love is to be selfless and sacrificial. Pursuing this kind of love gives us the *opportunity* to be "imitators of God," like Christ in our willingness to sacrifice for each other and be each other's servants. It also gives us the opportunity to know the comfort of a companion in the journey of knowing God. Knowing the kind of love that is necessary for marital fidelity is the beginning knowledge of how God loves us through Christ.

This completely contradicts what much of our current culture teaches, which is how important sex is in marriage, how sexual fulfillment indicates the health of a marriage, and that pursuing it is our inherent right. The biblical view seems to indicate that sex is not that important. In Rom. 12, Paul said, "Do not conform . . . to the pattern of this world." Perhaps part of renewing our minds is to develop a new attitude about sex. Perhaps the reason the Bible is silent about sexual practices is that it assumes we are more concerned about having a Christ-centered attitude about marriage and a Christlike relationship in marriage.

We are certainly not saying that sexual problems should not

be addressed and understood or that therapy shouldn't be used to alleviate any sexual problems. We are not saying sex is evil or dirty. (We will address some of these physical issues in the next chapter.) What does seem to be the case is that sex can be the expression of natural biological desires, but the biblical view is that sex needs to be in the deeper commitment and intimacy between a husband and wife.

> **Selflessness is the only way to get our needs met emotionally, spiritually, and physically.**

Emotional and spiritual intimacy between a husband and wife is very important. This intimacy is based on a Christlike attitude toward each other. It is an attitude of selflessness and service. When a couple achieves a mutual attitude about this, great sex might result. One great paradox of biblical faith is that when we are willing to give up something, we may get it back more powerfully than before.

For those who struggle with sexual temptation, selfish neediness fuels sexual lust. This neediness may be founded in experiences of being wounded. Loneliness and anger fuel selfish neediness. Anger about being deprived fuels rebellion.

Therefore, the antidote to sexual lust is working toward a greater Christlike selflessness. A simply way of looking at this could be as follows:

Selfishness = Normal Needs + Loneliness + Anger
Lust = Normal Sexual Desire + Selfishness
Infidelity = Normal Sexual Desire + Lust
Selflessness = A Life of Sacrifice and Service
Fidelity = Normal Sexual Desire + Selflessness

Selflessness is the only way to get our needs met emotionally, spiritually, and physically.

In the next six chapters we will expand this theory of healthy sexuality. We believe it is helpful to understand five dimensions that are important to being sexually whole.[1] These dimensions can clarify the challenges and hard work of remaining faithful.

In each dimension we will continue to illustrate the biblical perspective we have started here. The following diagram is a way to illustrate the dimensions, recognizing that four of them surround the most important one—spirituality. Spirituality will create the selflessness that is vital to sexual fidelity and wholeness.

HEALTHY SEXUALITY

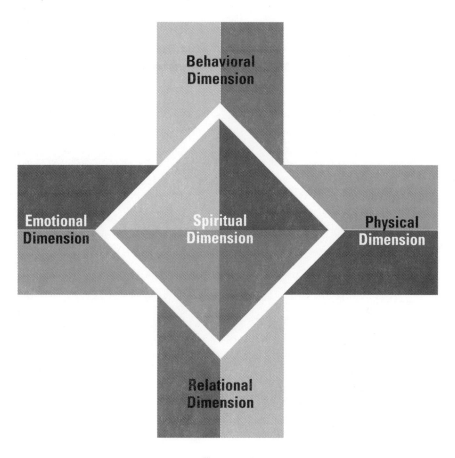

FIGURE 1

5

The Physical Dimension

Paul teaches in 1 Cor. 6:19-20, "Do you not know that your body is a temple of the Holy Spirit, who is in you, whom you have received from God? You are not your own; you were bought at a price. Therefore honor God with your body."

What an incredible scripture! It grounds us again in the theme that selflessness, realizing our bodies are not our own, is a key to sexual health. Although Paul's use of the word "body" is equivalent to the term "personality" or "self," it is a great statement regarding a Christian view of the human body's sacredness. This chapter wrestles with challenges in sexual functioning and physical self-care.

Too often impersonal sex happens not only outside of marriage but also within marriage. This brings acute loneliness for partners who long for deep closeness in which each act of physical intercourse reaffirms and renews an intimacy already there. A deep level of emotional and spiritual intercourse leads to satisfactory physical intercourse. The practice of tenderness and frequent, affectionate physical touching, combined with shared thoughts and feelings and a valuing of each other's bodies within the marriage, can lead to a deep mutual enjoyment.

The challenge for many couples in ministry is that they find emotional and physical areas of the relationship difficult to discuss. The relationship is painful when the sexual intimacy is disappointing or absent. Sexual frustration can lead to the search for intimacy in all the wrong places. Pornography and other forms of sexual sin are readily available to substitute for healthy intimacy and don't require the hard work necessary to sustain a relationship.

The physical dimension includes understanding how our bodies sexually function. Much sexual frustration in marriage is from a lack of information about human sexual response. We are fearfully and wonderfully made, and sexual response is an inherent part of that design.

Dr. Jack Anon's PLISSIT model of understanding both the diagnosis and treatment for sexual dysfunctions is tremendously helpful:

P—Permission to be sexual
LI—Limited information
SS—Specific suggestions
IT—Intensive therapy

Many Christians do not have "permission" to be sexual. They have heard only the don'ts—misinformation suggesting that all sexual behavior or even sexual thinking can inhibit a person's life.

> **Most adults grow up with "limited information" in sex education.**

Most adults grow up with "limited information" in sex education. "Specific suggestions" about physical intimacy are rarely found in the educational and worship experiences in most areas of our lives, including our churches. "Intensive therapy" may mean only that many of us pastors and our wives will need to become sexually educated so we can be healthy with each other and model that to others.

For their first years in marriage, Mark and Jodie, a young couple involved in youth ministry, enjoyed passionate sex. Mark had been sexual before his conversion to Christ, and Jodie was a virgin when they got married. Their sex lives were good after marriage. When Jodie got pregnant, they were overjoyed, but Jodie had a hard time physically. After the child was born, Jodie avoided sex. Mark became absorbed in his youth pastorate. Jodie threw herself into motherhood.

Neither Jodie nor Mark realized how deeply neglected Mark felt in the emotional and physical parts of the relationship. At times, Mark would use "soft" pornography and masturbate. He no longer cared if they had physical intercourse.

The couple continued to drift apart. Their wake-up call was when Mark became so flirtatious with a girl in his youth group that the girl's parents talked to the senior pastor. Mark was 26, and the girl was 18. Subsequently in couples therapy, Mark and Jodie dealt with the incredible pain of the physical and emotional intensity of Mark's flirtation with the girl.

Mark and Jodie's relationship, through prayer and their honest sharing with each other, including in therapy, led to the deepest level of intimacy they had experienced. Mark told the girl's parents in an "amends" process that he was grateful they had contacted his boss.

Mark and Jodie made it clear that revealing his behavior would probably best prevent his repeating the offense. Mark attended a weekly accountability group and called a sponsor whenever he was tempted to relapse.

"Limited information" about our bodies can damage our physical health. If we don't understand normal sexual response, we might be frightened by it. Romantic arousal, no matter what the source, affects our bodies. Our skin flushes, heartbeats quicken, heat spreads, and our state of consciousness is altered somewhat.

Those same hormones that can bring us together to love, marry, and bear children can also trick us into doing some pretty wild things. Many of us in ministry have performed actions we don't confide to anyone, even trusted friends. At times, the most dedicated Christian man or woman may behave abnormally. These behaviors couldn't be you or the person you believed yourself to be, or your spouse or the person you believed your spouse to be.

Physical arousal can be so powerful that it either can be a wonderful source of love and intimacy in a monogamous relationship or can lead to a choice to override common sense and a value system. Not only is it tough for a pastor to admit to using pornography, but it is also very difficult to talk about physical challenges, such as premature ejaculation, difficulty in getting and maintaining an erection, sexual anorexia, or any other physical problems common in the lives of couples in and out of ministry. Many clergy see physicians who are members of their own church and would never confide the embarrassment of physical challenges in a marriage.

Another challenge is that our culture supports the myth that males are always more sexual than females. This stereotype frequently puts even more pressure on the male pastor who does not have as much sexual drive as his wife. Although we have many more resources for sexual help than we had a decade ago, the fear of sharing sexual challenges does not seem to abate for many men and women in our culture.

Like the ebb and flow of the tides, many of our hormones rise and fall within our bodies in cycles. Depending on the triggering mechanism, a cycle might last a few minutes, a day, a week, a month, a season, a year, or a lifetime. It is not uncommon for couples to have not had physical intercourse for many months or several years. Learning that they're not alone in that experience is almost always amazing to such a couple.

Testosterone levels, for example, oscillate every 15-20 minutes in men and follow daily, seasonal, and annual rhythms. A pastor who does not understand this roller-coaster ride may feel threatened by the changes. This person's biological clock and emotional experiences, including family of origin, stress from church, and family life, can add to the challenges. Dr. Theresa L. Crenshaw writes, "Most of us realize that many women become irritable premenstrually, but not that more relationship conflicts occur at that time than at any other, and that it is probably the most common time for an argument to trigger a separation or divorce."[1]

Orgasm is a peak experience that some people enjoy more than others. Also depending on many variables, each person, in his or her own emotional and physical roller-coaster ride, has a variety of peak or valley experiences. A spouse usually cannot compete with the level of sexual intensity and arousal from the secret life of pornography.

James and Margaret had enjoyed fairly meaningful sex for more than 20 years. James had never used pornography until he stumbled across it on the Internet. Soon he was masturbating at least once a week to pornography and was initiating physical intercourse less frequently with Margaret. When Margaret asked him about the changes in their sexual behavior, he said that he had not noticed it.

After she brought that subject up, he tried to quit both the pornography and the masturbation but could not break the habit. Meanwhile, his wife heard a radio program on sexual addiction, including pornography. She sent for the tape of the program and asked him to listen to it. Even though Margaret did not know James was actually using Internet pornography, she was concerned about the major change in their sexual relationship and knew he spent much time on the

> **Intensive therapy experiences provide an opportunity to heal from the pain of sexual challenges in ministry couples' lives.**

Net. Her intuition told her maybe her husband had this problem or was vulnerable to such a possibility.

This incredible hunch paid off. James and Margaret subsequently came to therapy for a two-week intensive session. There he heard some other clergy members relate similar challenges in their lives, and kept in contact with one of them who became a role model for him. Margaret had a similar experience with a couple of women she met and with whom she continued phone contact. Intensive therapy experiences provide an opportunity to heal from the pain of sexual challenges in ministry couples' lives.

Sometimes simple, "specific suggestions" can help couples change dysfunctional sexual patterns. For example, one challenge involving the physical aspects of sexuality is determining which partner will initiate physical intercourse. Sometimes couples get pretty creative in this area. We know of several couples who have a candle in their bedroom. When one partner would like to have physical intercourse, he or she will light the candle. It can be devastating if the other partner enters the bedroom and blows out the candle, and the two of them do not talk about it. This can be fairly tragic when such an occurrence becomes one more time when the couple fails to communicate effectively.

The male is less likely to initiate physical intercourse when he has a problem getting or maintaining an erection. Again, failure to communicate leads to more time between sexual experiences.

Another common challenge is when one person is a "morning person" and the other is a "night person." Unless a husband and wife address differences such as this, their sexual intimacy might be diminished. The Wheats write, "Some people talk of marriage as ideally a 50/50 proposition. The problem with this idea is that each partner is always waiting for the other to do something first. With a 100/100 partnership, either partner acting with a 100 percent giving attitude will contribute to the total marriage, so that there will be a reciprocating love from the other partner."[2] Understanding this attitude is another simple change that can help.

One common challenge for couples in marital and sex therapy is to understand the "change first" principle, which suggests to each partner that he or she change himself or herself instead of waiting to see if the other partner changes. It is not unusual for one or the other partner, more frequently the male, to test the length of time between sexual intimacies without communicating this to the spouse.

One tool that can help individuals and couples who are experiencing physical dysfunction is to chart mood swings. For example, the female can chart relational conflicts and mood disorders for three months. She can then go back and compare these occurrences with her cycle.

It is also helpful for the male to chart for a three–month period of time arguments and other sources of tension in the marital relationship and compare this with work stressors and physical symptoms. Couples are sometimes amazed at the frequency of predictable reactions that they have not understood before.

The challenge for all of us is to apply the "Serenity Prayer," by Dr. Reinhold Niebuhr, to our sexual life through our different life stages: "God, grant me the serenity to accept the things I cannot change, courage to change the things I can, and the wisdom to know the difference." We must always talk about challenges in the area of physical intimacy with a safe person in order to receive the kind of help we need.

Dr. Patrick Carnes aides our understanding of sensuality: "Sensuousness requires stopping and paying attention. Once we do this, a new, deeper realm of experiences will open before us. Many religious and spiritual traditions recognize and acknowledge the connection between sensuality and spirituality. By truly opening to all that our senses bring us, we can become more open to and aware of the world around us—and thus we see the magnificence of creation."[3]

> **Many couples can heal sexual dysfunctions by simply learning how to communicate and by being willing to be creative.**

Most clergy do not really have a "Sabbath" experience in their own lives and seldom "smell the flowers." Unfortunately, most of us are better at *doing* than *being*. Physical and emotional challenges in sexuality occur in the rushing to be the kind of ministers, spouses, dads, or moms we believe we are expected to be—especially if we are perfectionistic.

We have described some general and limited hints as the PLISSIT model suggests. Many couples can heal sexual dysfunctions by simply learning how to communicate and by being willing to be creative. The last part of the model is "intensive therapy." This could refer to education about specific sexual information. Some very specific sexual dysfunctions may need intensive therapy from a medical doctor or sex therapist.

A couple experiencing sexual difficulties should have thorough medical evaluations. Some dysfunctions are biological in nature. Male diabetes, for example, can cause impotency. Medical interventions for this can be investigated. Problems with sexual desire can stem from a biological foundation. Some antidepressants, for example, can diminish sexual desire, and this should be discussed with the prescribing physician. The effective marketing campaign for drugs like Viagra reveals how common impotence is. Hormonal changes over time, as we discussed, can result from diet, exercise, and vitamin therapies.

The second reason for intensive therapy is to treat emotional factors. Many sexual dysfunctions have emotional foundations. Sometimes inhibited sexual desire can be directly linked to sexual abuse experiences. Impotence can be related to performance anxiety.

The case of Martha and Jerry illustrates another possible outcome of sexual abuse. Jerry's father sexually abused him when he was two. His mother also neglected to give Jerry love and nurture. As Jerry grew up, he got caught up in pornography searching for the female love and nurture he always wanted. When he married Martha, he hoped he could stop using pornography. When he couldn't, he assumed he needed to have more sex. He continually badgered Martha for more sex, as well as for creative ways of having it.

In treatment Jerry learned to stop his pornography habit. Martha, in therapy, learned that she should enjoy her own sexuality and not depend on Jerry to initiate sex. The therapist directed Martha to ask Jerry to let her initiate sex for 30 days.

The first night that Martha initiated, Jerry panicked and left the bedroom. Martha, feeling she had made a breakthrough, was shocked and angry. Jerry's abandonment issues had contributed to his pornography addiction and his aggressive sexual attitude. His sexual abuse experience contributed to his need to always initiate and be in control of sex. When his partner changed the pattern in a bedroom at night, he panicked because it triggered memories of his father harming him in his bedroom at night as a child.

When sex addiction or repetitive sexual sins have been the issue in a marriage, another physical factor needs to be addressed. We know the activity of the brain is chemical in nature. No nerve endings in the brain actually touch each other. Communication occurs as chemicals interact in the space between nerve endings. This is called neurochemistry. The various chemicals involved in this, called neurochemicals, are beginning to be identified. You might be familiar with two of them: serotonin and dopamine. Neurochemicals present in various parts of the brain can affect feelings of anxiety and depression. Various medications for anxiety and depression restore balances in neurochemistry.

Sexual fantasy and activity require various parts of the brain to communicate with each other to facilitate sexual response. The excitement of sex increases levels of adrenaline, the stress hormone, in the brain. It may also increase dopamine that has an antidepressant quality. In centers of the brain that cause feelings of sexual pleasure, hormones called catecholamines increase. Even looking at the picture of someone you love can elevate these pleasure hormones.

God has designed our brains (and our bodies) to react to all changes that occur in it. Our brains will seek to return to the normal state of balance. After we think about or perform sex, the neurochemicals involved will be restored to the normal balance. If a person continues to think about or perform some sexual activity, these neurochemicals will continually be elevated.

The brain will adjust eventually to this constant change. What was the normal balance will be modified upward over time. It's comparable to the case of blood pressure. If your blood pressure is normally 120/70 and you continually are stressed to the point that it is elevated to 170/110, your brain may establish that as the normal blood pressure. Now you will have to stop worrying or take medication to lower it.

Sex addicts are addicted to their own brain chemistry.

Alcoholics put a lot of alcohol into their bodies. Their brains will adjust to these changes. In time, they will need to put more alcohol into their brains to achieve the same effect. Their brains may even start "craving" this level and send messages that say, "I need another drink."

In medical language this is called tolerance. When sex becomes an addiction, this factor of tolerance is also operating. The brain has become used to a certain level of the chemistry of sex and will crave the same amount and eventually demand more to achieve the same effect.

In many ways, sex addicts are drug addicts. They are addicted to their own brain chemistry. As one colleague said, "Being a sex addict is like being an alcoholic if you were yourself a bar." Sex addicts have only to go to their fantasy lives to produce the supply in their brains.

This helps us realize that for a sex addict, there is no amount of sex that will always be enough. Their repetitive activities will always create a need for more sex and (in some cases) for new kinds. Their brains crave increased, and possibly the excitement of new, activities.

One sex addict owned the company that was the largest producer of pornographic videos in the world. This man had been sexual with thousands of women in thousands of ways. He said that it was never enough. He was never satisfied. He didn't find sexual satisfaction until he became a Christian, sold his company, and found a wife whom he loved. Now he has sex once or twice a week, and that is enough.

Sex addicts will also have to surrender any ideas that their spouses aren't available or attractive enough. The spouses, likewise, have to accept that the addiction is not about them, their appearance, or their performance. This is hard because of so many of our beliefs about sex.

When an alcoholic stops drinking, his or her brain will detoxify—which can sometimes be dramatic and cause violent physical reactions. A sex addict can also experience this effect to a lesser extent if he or she stops being sexual. However, sex addicts who are married won't stop being sexual forever. One therapy for sex addicts is that they agree to a period of total abstinence from one to three months. This allows the brain to readjust to a lower level of sexual demand and expectation.

A period of abstinence can also have emotional and spiritual benefits. It can teach the addict, and perhaps the spouse, that sex is not the most important need in their marriage. This strategy will work if a husband and wife agree to emphasize other aspects of their marriage. By doing this, they are telling themselves that their emotional and spiritual intimacy is more important than their sex lives.

Both husband and wife must agree with this plan as a positive exercise to restore normal neurochemical balance and to elevate emotional and spiritual intimacy. Paul says in 1 Cor. 7:5, "Do not deprive each other except by mutual consent and for a time, so that you may devote yourselves to prayer."

Couples react differently to this suggestion. Some addicts are angry. They wonder how they will maintain sobriety if they can't have sex. They feel this is yet another denial of their needs. If the theory of neurochemistry is correct, then the abstinence period will restore balance and the brain will eventually be satisfied with less. This makes fidelity easier and forces addicts to deal with their sense of abandonment. As they find fellowship for their loneliness and anger, their emotional need for sex will also decrease.

For the spouses of the addicts, a period of abstinence may come as a relief. They may be too angry to be sexual. Others may feel anxiety because they are operating with the same core beliefs. They believe that if their spouses don't have sex with them, the spouses might be more vulnerable to sexual temptation. This is not true. The spouses may also feel abandonment. They will wonder things such as, "What am I going to do? After all, my husband [or wife] has been out there having sex with everyone else and not me!"

Another very important aspect of the physical dimension is physical self-care. Seminaries don't always teach us to have a healthy physical lifestyle with a balance, including exercise, relaxation and rest, proper nutrition, and other important aspects of our lives that are not task related.

Dr. Howard Clinebell writes, "As a male, I have tended to allow oppressive cultural expectation for what it is to 'be a man' to fuel my work addiction; to prevent my developing fully my soft, vulnerable, feeling side; to limit my intimate involvement in the nurture of our children; and to make it difficult for me to nurture myself effectively. I continue to struggle to liberate myself from this culturally programmed self-oppression."[4]

The ability to resist sexual temptations will take energy. Healthy sexual expression in marriage will require energy. If we are chronically tired, we will be more vulnerable.

Self-affirmation is a vital part of physical self-care. Many couples struggle sexually perhaps because one or both partners don't consider themselves attractive.

Tom and Mary were an emotionally close young ministry couple. Mary was a twin but didn't look like her sister. Mary always thought she was the less attractive of the two. All through school, her tall, blond, socially outgoing sister got more attention. Mary felt like the "ugly duckling."

She was glad she found Tom but "knew" it wasn't because he was all that attracted to her physically. When Tom initiated sex, Mary thought it was just because all men need sex. After the honeymoon Mary began to find that her self-consciousness prevented her from really enjoying sex. She withdrew. As this happened, Tom grew angry but couldn't talk about it. During this time he discovered Internet pornography. He justified it to himself saying, "If Mary isn't available, these women on the Internet at least are. I can turn it on and off when I want to."

Both Tom and Mary were getting more and more lonely. When Mary discovered Tom's pornography habit, it confirmed in her mind that she wasn't as attractive as all these other women.

Mary's self-perception was a part of this problem. It is a common problem. Both authors have known Hollywood actresses who are desired by millions of men all over the world, but who felt the same way about themselves as Mary did. Many of them also suffered with sexual problems in their marriages, and some of them had eating disorders. Many of us have things about our bodies that we don't like. Some of these feelings go back to our childhood and adolescence. Perhaps we were teased or joked about. Some teasing can be cruel and leaves us with emotional scars. We looked at others and thought they were attractive and we weren't. We have forgotten we are "fearfully and wonderfully made" (Ps. 139:14). We may need to talk about these old wounds and ask God to help us heal.

To develop their relationship further, Tom will have to help Mary understand that she is beautiful to him and that this feeling is not about sex. Mary will need to accept that her sexual desires are normal and that it is OK to enjoy them. Both will need to heal from the betrayal of trust that Tom's pornography problem caused.

We must remember that God does want us to enjoy each other's bodies in marriage. It is a great gift. It is the way we find deeply intimate touch and affirmation. As Christians we should not be

afraid to admit our problems and talk about them and, in some cases, find help. For some people, physical self-perceptions and sexual
frustrations have led to many dysfunctional patterns, including the
possibility of sexual addiction.

In the next chapter we will explore the behavioral dimension.
We will need to understand this dimension in order to make any
changes in our behaviors necessary to bring us to health.

6

The Behavioral Dimension

This dimension considers the behaviors required to lead a faithful life. While the principles here apply to all areas of life, we will concentrate on sexuality.

Healthy sexuality demands that we stop medicating our feelings with sinful and addictive behaviors and get honest. Sexual addicts and sexual sinners fall into terrible habits and rituals.

Pastors, who may have every good intention, may let basic emotional and spiritual disciplines slide. They may have virtually no healthy boundaries. They are vulnerable in intimate ways with no one. Other people place them on pedestals, and they are afraid to come down and be human.

A pastor or anyone who wants to change will have to change many behaviors. Instead of rituals that lead to sexual sin, he or she will have to adopt new rituals that lead to healthy behaviors. After a lifetime of bad habits, good ones are easy to acquire.

David, for example, is the senior pastor of a large, successful church. He and his wife, Lisa, have a good marriage. Both, however, have become extremely busy—David with his preaching and administrative duties and Lisa with school teaching, their three children, and her role as pastor's wife. They are always coming and going and find it hard to take time for themselves with so many church demands.

David has hundreds of people who know him, but no real intimate friends. He prays with many others and conducts several Bible studies, but he is always the leader. His own prayer and study time has slid away. David has no real time for anything else. When various church matters are pressing, which is all the time, many things take a backseat. He hasn't met the other clergy in town for months. He and Lisa haven't had a night out since they can remember. Many elders oversee David's activity, but no one questions or monitors his daily routine.

One night, after a very long day, David checked his E-mail before going home. He didn't recognize one of the E-mails and opened it to find friendly content with an invitation to visit a web site. David clicked in and instantly faced the picture of nude women. He was shocked but also felt a rush of adrenalin and excitement. He closed the site but over the days and weeks returned to sites like this again and again. He told himself that he needed a little "relaxation." After all, his and Lisa's sex life has been boring and infrequent lately; maybe this will "spice things up."

Several months later the senior elder of his church came to him with a printout of items from the church computer.

David had become addicted to Internet pornography. He had no great trauma in his background and no major problems in his marriage. He was stressed out, tired, and never had anyone hold him accountable to his emotional and spiritual discipline. He was truly ignorant of how powerful pornography could be and fell into the trap. To get free of this he needed to set up a rigorous accountability program.

In a way, David became a "slave" to pornography. The concept of slavery reminds us of the story of the Jewish people in Num. 13 and 14. The Israelites were still in the desert after God had delivered them out of slavery in Egypt. Moses knew that God intended them to go to the Promised Land, so he sent one spy from each of Israel's 12 tribes to scout the land. Ten spies reported that the land was a great place but said, "We can't attack those people; they are stronger than we are."

These men "spread among the Israelites a bad report about the land." They also said, "The land we explored devours those living in it. All the people we saw there are of great size" (13:32).

After all the Jewish people had seen God do, you would think they would rebuke this report, knowing by faith that God would take them into the land. They were being led by Moses, who had talked to God directly. In Egypt, they had seen God send plagues against the most powerful man in the world, Pharaoh. They had crossed the Red Sea and watched as an entire army was destroyed. Despite this, their faith deserted them. Instead of having confidence, they all began to cry, "'If only we had died in Egypt! Or in this desert! Why is the LORD bringing us to this land only to let us fall by the sword? Our wives and children will be taken as plunder. Wouldn't it be better for us to go back to Egypt?' And they said to each other, 'We should choose a leader and go back to Egypt'" (14:2-4).

So they wanted to fire the man who led them so far and had talked to God. Moses and his brother Aaron were so discouraged that they fell on their faces in despair. It took the leader for the next generation, Joshua, to remind the people of their faith and eventually lead them to the land God promised them.

Sin and addiction are like this. We have seen the evidence of God's hand in our lives, but when we face tests of our faith, it is easy to return to ways we know. Addictive or destructive behaviors might be the most familiar things to us. We may have been raised with them. Our "Egypt," our slavery to destructive behaviors, is what we know. We might think it is better to return to what we know than to face unseen dangers or challenges in the future. Our proud nature, which is afraid to admit we are sinners, tells us not to face risk.

We need strong leadership, support, encouragement, and accountability.

Given this temptation and fear, it is hard to change our ways. We lack leaders we can be honest with who will show us the way. Where is Joshua today?

One of our first encouragements for you is to stop beating yourself if you have had a hard time changing your sinful and destructive behaviors. If the Jewish people couldn't handle their fears despite what they had seen, how can we expect more of ourselves? Instead, we need guides and principles to follow to allay our fears. We will need strong leadership, support, encouragement, and accountability.

The story of Nehemiah is a great biblical teaching about accountability. Nehemiah was a Jewish captive in Susa after the Babylonians overran Israel. Nehemiah was set in place as cupbearer to the king. This was an important job. You at least get to hang out with the king in the throne room, a room of great power. Nehemiah's brother Hanani and some other men traveled 1000 miles from Jerusalem to meet with Nehemiah. They were distressed because the walls of Jerusalem were broken down and the gates destroyed by fire (Neh. 1:3).

The report of the city is like some of our lives—the city of our lives is in ruin, rubble. The gates in and out of our minds and hearts have been destroyed by fire.

Nehemiah was destined to be a great leader. Perhaps when we

think of a great leader, we might imagine someone who has mastered Stephen Covey's "Seven Habits of Highly Effective People." We might want someone to assert himself or herself, to be dramatic and powerful. However, our great leader, Nehemiah, responded this way: "When I heard these things, I sat down and wept" (v. 4).

How many of us have kept our emotions bottled up inside? We have refused to cry or to be sad, thinking it is immature or not Christian. To begin the trek to great leadership, we must be honest about our feelings.

Great leadership begins with prayer. Nehemiah prayed a very basic prayer (vv. 7-11) that says in part, "God, You said that if we stray from Your path, You would scatter us to the nations" (author's paraphrase).

The consequences of a sinful life can leave us feeling pretty scattered. Nehemiah's prayer also says, "Remember God . . ." Do you like the prayers in the Bible where we remind God of things? Isn't that interesting? It's as if God needs to be reminded. Nehemiah basically said, "Remember God, You promised us that if we returned to You, You would return us to home." That's the prayer.

Nehemiah still didn't have an idea what he wanted to do, what his strategy would be. He had no vision or plan. He only had desire and humility. He wanted to go home.

In the second chapter, King Artaxerxes seemed to be a master psychologist. Nehemiah prepared the cup for the king, took it into him, drank it, and didn't die, so the king was ready to drink it. Then the king said to Nehemiah, "You look sad." Has anyone ever said that to you? "You look really sad." The king observed that Nehemiah didn't look as if he were ailing physically, so it must be sadness of heart.

Many of us who have been in trouble with sexual sin think we can get well alone.

Nehemiah said, "Why should my face not look sad when the city where my fathers are buried lies in ruins, and its gates have been destroyed by fire?" (Neh. 2:3).

In other words, he says, "Why shouldn't I be feeling this way!" Sometimes when we simply state our feelings, even our sadness and anger, someone may have the right response. The king, a very wise man, asked, "What do you need?" Nehemiah said, "I want to go home! I want some letters of reference!"

Next Nehemiah was about to make the main mistake of those who want to get well. He decided, "I will make a 1,000-mile journey on foot with letters of recommendation *by myself.*" Many of us who have been in trouble with sexual sin think we can get well alone. We might even think we can do it with God's help, but without the help of others. This is actually a rather grandiose thought, and we are really saying, "I don't need help."

The king is wiser, and in verse 9, Nehemiah reports that the king also sent the cavalry and army officers with him. The king knew he needed protection and fellowship in order to make that journey. Why? The end of chapter 2 shows us that Nehemiah would face enemies on this journey, including Sanballat the Horonite. The enemies ridiculed the fact that Nehemiah was returning to do something about the destruction of the city.

How about in the city of your life? Some people will not like the fact that you are coming home. They like the status quo. They may have laid claim to lands that are rightfully yours. They are somehow invested in your failures.

Even though we make the right decisions to get well and return to God, we still must remember the journey of healing has only just begun. Enemies will attack. Life is like that.

The close of chapter 2 describes how Nehemiah began to survey the damage of the city. He went out at night, embarrassed, ashamed, and sad because of what had happened. In the early days of Alcoholics Anonymous, meeting times were always set to begin after the sun went down. This was the procedure because those attending didn't want anyone to see them go into the meeting.

The early days, weeks, and months of a healing journey may be like this. When we become humble about our sins, we wake up to damage that we've done. We've been medicating pain and damage for years. We've been spacing it out, disassociating from it, denying it, and repressing it. Suddenly we get sober and see what we've done.

Nehemiah got a picture of the great state of disrepair and despair the city was in. The work must have seemed overwhelming. Another common mistake many Christians make is thinking that because they've decided to do the right thing and get well, God will automatically make everything right. They think God will perform some miracle and help them avoid all consequences of their bad decisions. The fact that consequences still happen and that the work is long may discourage many.

Nehemiah did the right thing at the end of chapter 2. He didn't make a grand and glorious speech. He simply gathered the leaders and said, "Let's start building." Nobody really needed to get super motivated. Nobody needed to rush out with a grand vision looking for the golden trowel. They all simply needed a word of direction and encouragement, "Let's get started" (paraphrased).

Chapter 3 is a great chapter about organization. Different families and groups of people were assigned to sections of the wall. One obvious principle is that when you're tackling a massive project, break it into smaller and more manageable parts.

Two other principles are tucked away in this chapter. In verse 10, Jedaiah built a section of wall directly across from his house. That is a wonderful image. Many people, notably pastors, are tempted to rush out and save the world. They try to build things all over the place. This verse reminds us to stay close to home, to get things right in our own worlds first.

When Mark Laaser was in treatment for sexual addiction, he heard Pat Carnes speak one night. He felt a burst of energy propelling him to go out and speak and save the world from sexual addiction. Pat gently reminded him that first he needed to go home and get a year of sobriety before he thought about speaking to anyone else.

That is a great reminder. We need to be whole ourselves before we try to help someone else. So many pastors and Christian caregivers have great hearts about helping others but are not well themselves. Instead of being "wounded healers" as Henry Nouwen described, they are really "unhealed wounders." They take care of others to avoid their own issues. This chapter reminds us to build close to home.

A third principle of this chapter appears in verse 14. Malkijah was assigned to repair the "Dung Gate." All of the garbage and waste of the city was disposed of through this gate. It might seem like a lowly assignment—"We get to work with dung!" Sometimes life seems like that—we have a whole lot of waste to deal with.

However, this may be one of the most important gates of the city. A city without a sanitation system will choke on its own pollution. During the American Civil War one of the greatest challenges of moving a large army was figuring out a latrine system. Have you ever been in a large city during a sanitation strike?

Perhaps one of the greatest medical advances of the 20th century was the development of sanitation systems. This was possibly even more important than the invention of penicillin. The Dung Gate was an important gate. Sometimes the dirtiest, smelliest work is like that. We all need to get pollution and waste out of our lives. This could be the waste of unhealed memories, past sins, or painful feelings. Open the gate to your heart, and ask God what things you may need to get out.

Chapter 4 begins with the Jews' enemies ridiculing them about their work. Sanballat and his friend Tobiah asked, "What are those feeble Jews doing? . . . Can they bring the stones back to life from those heaps of rubble—burned as they are?" (v. 2).

> **We should know the enemy will attack and we should be ready.**

This is not only the voice of others who doubt us based on our history but also the voice of our own doubt. Can we rebuild or restore lives, marriages, and jobs? These will be the voices of early recovery. The work is ominous and long. The destruction seems complete. What can we really do?

Nehemiah must have ignored these taunts because the next thing we read is that the work was getting done. When the enemies learned the wall was getting built, they began to plot to come against it militarily. Nehemiah knew this. Much of chapter 4 describes the preparation. So Nehemiah stationed guards day and night.

Those of us struggling with sexual temptation need to be guarded day and night. We should know the enemy will attack and we should be ready. Our preparations must be secure. In 1 Pet. 5:8 Peter encourages us: "Be self-controlled and alert. Your enemy the devil prowls around like a roaring lion looking for someone to devour."

You need to have some warriors on guard day and night. This is another great principle of accountability. Prepare in times of strength for those times of weakness and attack that will come. Many who fail think that they can wait until temptation comes and then make a call. They assume they will be strong enough to resist. This is pride talking, not humility. They think they can somehow prove their worthiness to God by being strong. Instead, God asks us to trust Him enough to let others around us help stand guard.

When sex addicts go on a trip, for example, they can't rely on the fact that they will call someone if they get tempted. They must prepare for those times of relative tiredness and stress when they might not be strong enough on their own to even make a call. They ask others to call them. They are aware of when they are more vulnerable and plan accordingly. Even when they get to hotels in other cities, when they are relatively strong checking in, they will ask front desks to cut off the cable channels in their rooms that might carry pornography.

Peter also says in 1 Pet. 5:9, "Resist him, standing firm in the faith, because you know that your brothers throughout the world are undergoing the same kind of sufferings."

Other men and women are facing the same struggles that we are. We need each other. In Neh. 4:13, Nehemiah tells of posting guards day and night by families. Families, communities of people, are the main foundations of strength.

In verse 16, Nehemiah says from that day, half the people built and half stood guard or defended the project. This illustrates another great principle. One great mistake about accountability is thinking that it is only about defense. We must also have accountability about building.

In recovery, we must also have an idea of what we are building. Is it our faith, our marriages, our careers? Some recent writers have reminded us that we need to have a vision. As Christians we must have a sense of our calling, our talents, and our gifts.

Some of us get stuck in recovery just defending. Afraid, we try to avoid the next terrible consequence. Some of us get stuck with just building and forget to defend. If we only build, we will be destroyed by the attack. If we only defend, we will go no place. In Neh. 4:17 we read that even the half who built carried a sword in one hand and a trowel in the other. Building, defending, building, defending, that's what recovery is all about—24/7, day and night.

This picture of preparation shows that all were involved in this community endeavor. Another great mistake many Christians make is in thinking that accountability is with only one other person. You decide you will report to one man or woman who will hold you accountable. However, what if this one person, your ultimate true friend who really understands you, needs a vacation and is out of town. You call this person up, and he or she is not there. Your loneliness may have triggered your sexual temptation in the first place. You feel angry. You may be tempted to think, "Well, if my accountability partner is not available, what am I supposed to do?"

One person is not enough. We need the "warriors," plural, around us all the time. Everyone in recovery needs a group or fellowship. Who are the warriors in your life?

You need a list. Let's say that one person is not home or is not available. Another person does not feel like talking to you today. You need to have a list, a community of those who will fight with you.

Another mistake Christians can make is to think it is possible to wait for temptation to strike before reaching out for help. Remember, Nehemiah teaches us that this is an all-day, everyday plan. Nehemiah tells us to prepare in the times of strength, knowing that times of weakness will come.

At times we will be tired, lonely, angry, and depleted. When we feel like that, we don't feel like reaching out. We may not want anyone to intervene with us. We must ask others to call us or reach out to us whether we like it or not. When our strength tells us we want to be faithful, that is when we should create the plan of support that will operate even when we don't feel like staying true to it.

Dan went to a meeting every Sunday night for those struggling with sex addiction. On the way to his meeting he passed a road that led to strip clubs and massage parlors. Every week he struggled with turning down that road. Several nights he did. Dan needed to either take a different road to the meeting or ask someone to ride with him. A necessary plan will not be hard to understand. We must choose it when we are strong and put it into place for those times when we are weak.

> **What legacy do you want to pass on to your children?**

Finally, listen to the great battle cry. Nehemiah says in 4:14, "Remember the Lord, who is . . . awesome." We all need to start with this realization. God can win this battle. Nehemiah tells his listeners to hear these words "and fight for your brothers, your sons and your daughters, your wives and your homes."

Nehemiah reminds the warriors whom the battle is for. The battle belongs to God and should be fought for others. If your recovery is only selfishly motivated, you will fail. If you are only trying to avoid consequences and are motivated by fear, you will not succeed.

The fight is for your wives, for your husbands. Do you really want to hurt them again? Or do you consider yourselves to be the guardians of their hearts? The fight is for your sons. What legacy do you want to pass on to them? The fight is for your daughters. What legacy do you want young women to know about being a young woman? Do you want them to think they are sex objects to be ogled in pornography or to be sexually manipulated? The fight is for your brothers and your sisters. They are the ones wondering where the next pornographic fix is, where the next strip club is located, when they will get enough money for the next prostitute, or who their next affair partner will be. These people are all around us. All of our fights should be for them. Are you willing to battle for those who are still struggling?

That is what recovery is about—carrying the message to others. This is like all great spiritual paradoxs. If you infuse energy into recovery for others, you will find benefit. Paul teaches us in Eph. 5:1-3, "Be imitators of God, therefore, as dearly loved children and live a life of love, just as Christ loved us and gave himself up for us as a fragrant offering and sacrifice to God. But among you there must not be even a hint of sexual immorality, or of any kind of impurity, or of greed, because these are improper for God's holy people."

Notice how Paul prefaces a warning about sexual immorality by teaching us to imitate God and to live a sacrificial life like Christ's. Living a life of service to others can be one of the best ways to motivate recovery.

Nehemiah 5 says the building project got expensive. With the wall reaching half its height, the bricks and the mortar were expensive and people were going into debt.

Do you battle with compulsive debt? Many who struggle with sexual temptation also struggle with money. Recovery can be expensive, as you wonder how you'll pay for therapy sessions and workshops and retreats. At times you will get into debt doing the right thing for yourself.

Do you know what the Jewish people did in those days? They sold their children into slavery. Nehemiah had to buy them back. Sometimes you wonder how you can spend time for yourself going to meetings and counseling. You might ask, "Am I abandoning my children?" The only way to leave a lasting and healthy legacy for your children is to get help for yourself.

Others in the city were figuring out ways to profit from the work. Nehemiah calls it "usury" (v. 7). Beware of people in your life who would profit from your mistakes or your desire to get well. Recovery will be expensive. Trust God. Spend the money—not foolishly, but consider it the best investment you can make.

Finally, in chapter 6, the wall was getting finished. The only work left was to put the doors and bolts in place. Sanballet and Tobiah knew that a direct frontal assault would fail. Somehow they must get Nehemiah off the wall and possibly out of the city. In this chapter they devised three strategies to do so. The first plan was to meet outside of the city. With what appeared to be a spirit of friendship, they set up a tent and invited Nehemiah to come into the tent and meet with them. They were, however, plotting to kill him.

Nehemiah must have been tempted to take a break from the hard work and relax. He might have also been tempted to want to end the hostility with some reconciliation, a peace process.

Likewise, at a point for those of us in recovery, it seems tempting to take a break from the work of maintaining a strong wall of defense. The enemies aren't really so bad; maybe we should make friends with them. Sometimes we feel restricted by having to stay behind the walls, inside the boundaries. Often the worst time of vulnerability for those in recovery is between 6 and 18 months.

But Nehemiah said, "I don't have time for this meeting, don't bother me from my important work!" We need to trust that our work, however tiring, boring, or mundane it may seem, needs to continue. We also need to recognize that we will feel "different." We might think other men and women don't struggle with these issues, so why do we have to be so protected and restricted? These are vulnerable feelings. We will need warriors around us to remind us to continue the work.

The second plot to get Nehemiah away from his work was the most sinister. The enemies circulated a false rumor (v. 6) that Nehemiah was planning a revolt and wanted to be king! They were basically saying that he was trying to be too important and needed to be brought down. That he was a threat to the king of Babylon. In the New Testament, this strategy, using the same type of rumor and false report, was used to have Jesus arrested.

Nehemiah had a very quick response. He basically said (v. 8), "You're making that up! I'm not coming down."

If any of us seek to recover from sexual sin and temptation and are trying to build more faithful lives, we can be sure that many will not understand. They may possibly even accuse us of false actions and beliefs. People might wonder who we think we are. They may accuse us of being self-righteous. People may be jealous of our success and just be waiting for us to make a mistake. Misery loves company.

On some days, people won't understand why you have to go to meetings or counseling or why you won't engage in certain activities. "Why won't you have cable TV in your home, because you yourself are tempted?" You may feel tired of being misunderstood or considered "strange." Remember the image of Nehemiah standing on the wall saying, "I'm not coming down—give me another brick."

The last strategy Sanballat and the other enemies created was from Shemaiah, who was an invalid. He told Nehemiah, "It's dangerous on the wall. Men are trying to kill you. Why don't you come with me to the Temple where we can be safe?" (see v. 10).

How many of you on Sunday morning know some temple dwellers who are in your church services to be safe but who would not consider taking their faith into a dangerous world?

At times, doing the right thing for your protection or your recovery will not seem very safe. For one thing, telling others the truth about your life is pretty risky. To be accountable to others, you will have to tell them about your past, your temptations, and your feelings. Accountability is about true intimacy. Intimacy means you are honest about yourself.

Imagine, for example, that you are at a shopping mall. The average mall offers lots of sexual stimuli these days. Let's say you are with a group of friends, maybe even a group from your church. You might say you are in accountability by being in this group. Let's say you are sexually tempted by something stimulating there but are too afraid to talk about it. Your silence will feed the power of that temptation. It might fester and grow.

Imagine, on the other hand, that you are at the same mall and encounter the same temptation, but the people with you know your story. This is a group with whom you

One of the greatest contributors to sexual sin is loneliness.

share your most intimate history, thoughts, temptations, and struggles. It will be natural for you to share the current temptation you are experiencing. Doing that with this group will take the power of the temptation away.

Remember, one of the greatest contributors to sexual sin is loneliness. Taking the risk to be honest is one of the greatest defenses against temptation. The principle here is that you must be in intimate accountability. Accountability must be with people who know you. This kind of fellowship helps you feel less lonely, which has a preventive effect. Intimate fellowship with other Christians will usually free you from lustful thoughts and temptations. It is risky to be that honest. Many churches in America are filled with people who are being safe and not getting honest?

Stay up on the wall. God is our protection. When we work patiently, success might not be as far away as we think. The rebuilding of the wall of Jerusalem took only 52 days (v. 15).

In summary, here are the basic principles of accountability in Nehemiah:

1. We can't recover alone. Recovery is a long journey, and we will need a community of warriors around us.

2. A community doesn't mean just one other person. It means groups of people stationed at the weakest places of our lives.

3. We can't wait for temptation to strike. We must prepare in times of strength and commitment for those times of attack that we know will come.

4. We must be accountable both to defend against the attack and to build a better life into the future. These two activities must be in equal measure.

5. Being accountable means being totally honest. This is the only path to intimacy; intimacy is the only way to feel less lonely. The fellowship of accountability brings freedom from lustful thoughts and temptations.

6. Our motivation for recovery should be to serve others and ourselves.

7. We will get tired, get distracted, and pity ourselves. We must ask God for strength to stay at the task one day at a time.

How does a pastor or anyone find fellowship? In the next chapter we will explain the emotional dimension of healthy sexuality and the work necessary to be available for fellowship.

7

The Emotional Dimension

We believe powerful emotions underlie a pastor's use of pornography. The pastor's unresolved emotional conflicts may hold seeds for sexual sin. He or she may not fully realize this. A pastor may feel a leader cannot have such problems. The fear of not being perfect can lead to attempts to explain away seeds of sin or to deny that they exist.

A clergy member must deceive himself or herself to indulge in pornography. This leads to a double life. The pastor may seem to lead an exemplary life, even to his or her own family. However, inside, consciously and unconsciously, he or she may be lonely, depressed, anxious, afraid, and angry.

This chapter will help us look at how a minister can lead a double life. Henry Ward Beecher said, "Excuses of moral delinquency are, therefore, usually processes of self-deception. At first they may not be; but at length a man who tries to deceive himself comes into that state in which he can do nothing else but deceive himself. A man can put out his eyes, inwardly, so that at last he will not see that a lie is a lie, and a truth a truth."[1]

Many of us have gone to church for a lifetime trying to impress those around us with how well we're doing. We wouldn't want to admit we have problems for fear of being judged as inferior Christians. Unfortunately, few seminaries help us deal with that dynamic.

Marilyn Murray has developed the following theoretical model we have used with pastors, the "Scindo Syndrome."[2] This categorizes six ways we might react to emotional pain. As you read the definitions, explore these dimensions in your life.

Original Feeling Child

This is the person you were created to be at birth. Your soul/true spirituality is the core of this.

As years pass, we often lose who we are inside. As we grow

up, we are taught to hide our feelings and are frequently asked to focus on our cognitive, thinking, abilities more and to make our feelings, or the affective side of our lives, less important. The elements and challenges in our lives do not encourage us to develop our individuality. Very few clergy would say church leadership encourages spontaneity and the honest expression of feelings.

Sobbing Hurting Child

Your "pool of pain," created by outside negative influences (abuse, neglect, illness, etc.), contains painful feelings (fear, sadness, anger, loneliness, helplessness, etc.). The positive side is that these experience may enable you to feel empathy and compassion, to be tender and caring.

> **Hiding from pain can enable us to seek an escape from or medication for emotions.**

Most pastors have an enormous "pool of pain" in their lives. We are bombarded with studies that indicate the anger and identify the confusion, feelings of betrayal, and underlying hurt that appear to consume most of those in the pastoral field.

Hiding from pain can enable us to seek an escape from or medication for emotions, of which we are sometimes not even aware.

Samuel had been in ministry for approximately 20 years when he started therapy because he used pornography. After Samuel had started viewing pornography, he started visiting child-porn sites. The next step was when he stopped at a playground and sexually fantasized about a couple of the children. His wake-up call was when an adult approached him to see if she "could help him." He felt that the woman was wondering why he was there, and he realized this person could have easily been a member of his church or someone who knew him.

He courageously talked about this event with his best friend, who suggested that he get some counseling. During therapy, Samuel dealt with much internal pain from his childhood, and with his role as a pastor. As he delved into the pains he held inside, for the first time, he begin to experience some healing.

One aspect of his therapy became vocational counseling when he realized he might never have entered the ministry if he had dealt with his pain before seminary. He said he had never experienced a calling from God but had felt driven by his pain to enter ministry.

Controlling Child

Sometimes you may become controlling to hold down your pain. Some common defenses are repression; anesthetizing (food, alcohol, drugs, sex, tobacco); and diversionary tactics (relationships, school, work, church, sports, music, reading, television, computers, etc.).

As a defense mechanism your "controlling child" is meant to be a *temporary* help in time of pain and distress. Your controlling child also keeps you responsible and helps you set healthy boundaries (keeps others from victimizing you and keeps you from victimizing others).

This appears to be where most pastors spend their lives. The rigors of being a minister are a set up to live in the world of control. Many clergy are "control addicts." Since most pastors are not taught to deal with their pain, they have many ways to control their emotions.

Most pastors' work schedules are so out of balance that they will not pay attention to what's going on inside them. Therefore, they tend not to take care of themselves emotionally. When there is no balance in the their lives, the potential for anesthetizing is heightened. For clergy the drugs of work, sex, food, alcohol, or substance abuse can provide an escape.

Matt was the senior pastor of a large congregation. He had been a successful athlete in college and had done well academically. So Matt was disciplined throughout seminary. Then his career fast-laned into a very successful pastorate. Matt worked seven days a week and seldom took a day off. He first encountered pornography when a young man in his church came to him for help in combating his own use of pornography. Matt checked out some porn on the Internet. To his amazement, he quickly developed a pornography habit that he couldn't stop. He was soon involved in cybersex at least two to three times a week. His only time-outs from his incredible work schedule were the pornographic interludes.

Matt's shame mushroomed as he dealt with his Jekyll-and-Hyde life. His turning point came when he became responsible for handling the consequences for a colleague who had had multiple affairs. He confessed his use of pornography to a therapist and friend. This person suggested that he seek professional help. In therapy, Matt realized his inner life had been out of control for many years, despite his illusion of control. He had never let himself pay attention to his feelings and their effect in his life. Matt began a process of healing, which eventually enriched his personal and professional life.

Therapy with his wife also helped Matt understand how much he had damaged his marriage by not giving himself or his spouse prime time. His wife had felt abandoned and had neglected her feelings by leading a women's Bible study group. They realized they had both helped others at the expense of their own marriage.

Matt also discovered how he'd hurt his two children by not being available to them emotionally. He attended their school activities, but he neglected their internal challenges. Family therapy helped him bridge this gap.

When Matt began therapy for one problem, he found the floodgates opened. Another unintended, but wonderful, consequence of his therapy was that his relationship with Christ took on new dimensions.

Feeling Adult

This is the "goal" in the healing journey of recovery: the integrated person—rational, reasonable, thinking, responsible, but deeply connected with feelings. This is the mature person who can experience feelings appropriately.

It is unlikely that anyone achieves perfection in the goal of being a "feeling adult." But Jesus' life represents a role model. The Gospels show us examples where Jesus knew His own feelings and responded to the feelings of people around Him. When His words in John 8:7 state "If any one of you is without sin, let him be the first to throw a stone at her," He was being very sensitive to the data and feelings in that situation. Instead of being judgmental, He opted for a caring position. This integration of the mind and emotions is difficult to achieve.

When pastors turn to pornography, they are not functioning as mature people, appropriately dealing with all of their feelings, nor are they making correct choices.

Angry Rebellious Child

This person is overtly hostile, resembling two electrical live wires connecting. You'll find this person to be aggressive, demanding, stubborn, and quick to blow up. ("Don't tell *me* what to do!" "I'll do it *my* way!" "I don't care what you think!")

Certainly many of us have temper tantrums, such as those who blow up in board or staff meetings. When the attitudes of "I'll do it my way" and "I don't care what you think" are the approach of a clergy person or lay leader, watch for the fireworks.

Joe discovered that pornography became a way he responded to his anger toward Jeff, a church member with whom he had an ongoing power struggle. After one meeting in which Joe and Jeff had yelled at each other, Joe realized his use of pornography and masturbation a few hours later was linked to his hostility toward Jeff. In therapy, he realized that this pattern had followed him from early adolescence into his years as a minister.

The Stubborn Selfish Child

This person is covert, passive-aggressive, and is a manipulator. He or she plays games; is sneaky, revengeful, grandiose; and can be seductive or promiscuous. ("I deserve this." "Whatever feels good, do it!")

This person is unreasonable; will rationalize to justify behavior; won't look at the consequences of actions; and refuses to take responsibility, usually blaming others. People like this will also do whatever they want even though they know their actions will destroy themselves and others. They see themselves as the victims but victimize themselves or others.

Addictions are born here!

Realizing this helps us understand the seeds of a pastor's use of pornography. How many of us pastors will admit we are stubborn or selfish? Pornography provides an unhealthy resource for this kind of person. Such a pastor feels a sense of entitlement. "I deserve this because I spend so much time in the Lord's service" is a common rationalization. This person tends to blame others and other things—including spouses and challenges in their ministry—for his or her inappropriate actions.

Chuck was unhappy in his marriage and in his ministry. He saw himself as the victim in both arenas. He continually argued with his wife, who, he believed, did not nurture him enough. And he felt overwhelmed by the additional responsibilities of the parish life.

Chuck discovered that pornography took him to an altered state of consciousness, which he felt was more successful for him than prayer or reading Scripture. So pornography became a daily ritual. But his double life also caused acute depression and suicidal thoughts. He entered therapy because of depression and told his therapist about his porn use. Through therapy, Chuck found marital health and a new way to deal with his ministry frustrations. He stopped using pornography.

> **Change does not occur without asking God and others for help.**

We hope these definitions will help you analyze and get help for your own challenges. Fortunately, all of us can change and be delivered from the bondage of sexual sin. However, change does not occur without asking God and others for help. As the case illustrations have shown, we often have to undergo much personal work and therapy to grow in understanding and in emotional and spiritual maturity.

To help you understand the reasons behind your pornographic use and addictions, Dr. Patrick Carnes has written about how people cope with trauma and the resulting wounds from their past. In *The Betrayal Bond*, he has listed ways that many of us have used to cope with trauma:[3]

1. **Trauma Reactions.** These occur when your mind, body, or spirit tells you that you are afraid. You might have anxiety, panic attacks, and vivid, disturbing dreams. Any of these might be especially frightening because they may not seem to have a cause. This is especially true if you don't consciously remember the original trauma. The stress of anxiety takes a toll on your body through aches and pains. Spiritually you might feel that God has abandoned you.

2. **Trauma Repetition**. This involves a pattern of repeating old behaviors. Have you ever said to yourself, "Why am I doing that again?"? Sometimes we are unconsciously hoping for a different result. Sometimes we replay the scenario and try to be in the controlling position. With sexual abuse, for example, we can replay abusive situations with either strategy.

3. **Trauma Bonds**. In this model people attempt to be in re-

lationships that allow them to replay old patterns. It is as if they need fellow actors to recreate the scenes. This model explains why some people, such as domestic-abuse survivors, return to abusive relationships. They are hoping for different results or miraculous resolutions. At other times people seek relationships that allow them to be the aggressors or abusive partners.

4. Trauma Shame. This pattern creates shame-based people. Their wounds have convinced them that they are worthless, and they grow accustomed to the role. They act depressed and needy but as if they don't want any help. It is frustrating to try to help them because large parts of them don't want to get well.

5. Trauma Pleasure. In this pattern people find some pleasure or excitement in being wounded. There is a variety of reasons for this. If the only attention they have ever received is to be mistreated, they will repeat the pattern to get attention. Sex-abuse survivors may know that the only time they were touched was to be molested. No touching is worse than some, so they seek the same kind of sexual relationships. This dynamic, partly, explains the phenomenon of sadomasochism. These are people who seem to enjoy being tortured and humiliated. We should also recognize that nothing is black and white. While early sexual abuse might have been painful and frightening, it might simultaneously have been sexually exciting. When these two dynamics collide, it can set people up to repeat the pattern to find the same excitement.

6. Trauma Blocking. This is any effort a person makes to numb the pain of trauma. The most obvious way to do so is to alter feelings with chemicals such as alcohol, cocaine, heroin, caffeine, and nicotine. Sexual fantasy can alter feelings, as can a variety of behaviors that have the capability to change brain chemistry. Changing feelings can mean that a person seeks to raise or lower his or her mood.

7. Trauma Splitting. This pattern means a person doesn't need a chemical or behavior to change how he or she feels. A person who splits can simply "leave" or disassociate from the situation. A person in this state can appear numb, distant, distracted, or unaware. In severe cases a person can even seem to have different personalities. Rape victims, for example, feel they are able to leave their bodies. When a person is in such pain, his or her conscious mind can't tolerate the thoughts that trigger the pain. In simpler cases this pattern may simply mean that a person denies or refuses to accept his or her level of loneliness, depression, anxiety, or fear.

8. Trauma Abstinence. This pattern causes people to avoid any thoughts or behaviors that remind them of their pain. These people lead a life of some avoidance or deprivation. The World War II generation lived through the trauma of a depression and a world war. Many of these people had great trauma about not having "enough." They saved everything and certainly don't suffer from the same need to self-indulge that younger generations do. This is not so bad except when it causes them to not spend money on what they need or would enjoy. Many of them are leaving behind great wealth.

Some people have great pain from the past about their appearance. They may starve themselves (anorexia) to assure themselves that they are in control of their weight. Those who are sexually abused may avoid sex (sexual anorexia) so they won't be reminded of that pain. Some people don't even like going outside because the world in general makes them too anxious (agoraphobia).

Recovering from any of these trauma reactions is a journey of healing. This is not an easy process and requires courage and a willingness to encounter the pain of the original wound. We believe it involves understanding the pain of the original wound. In most cases this means going back to childhood memories. We would suggest the following key elements of a healing journey:

1. Find a safe place to heal and safe people to heal with. Those who are afraid to be vulnerable to the pain of their feelings should find safe places to do so. Unfortunately, many people don't experience churches as safe places. It can be frightening to be honest at church for fear of what others will think. This is particularly true for pastors. This is why therapists and support groups have seemed safer. A safe place is one where we can be honest without fear of judgment.

Often this happens when others in the group are also able to be honest. Safe people may have lived through similar struggles and, out of their common brokenness, can be affirming and accepting.

2. Allow yourself to go back to the child. Whether we like it or not, each of us has a child inside. Developmental psychologists say we are as old as our last developmental accomplishments. Many of us act three or four years old at times, having a temper tantrum or being needy. Most of us have stored memories and can instantly get triggered into the feelings associated with them. Most of us need safe and skilled people to guide us in the task of knowing those memories and feelings. At the end of this chapter we will detail an exercise that might help you discern what your sexual and romantic fantasies might be telling you about your wounds.

3. Recognize and accept your anger. Christians are sometimes afraid of their anger. Expressing anger seems consistent with the biblical witness. The Book of Psalms alone should convince us that great anger could be followed by tremendous affirmations of faith. Jesus, himself, got angry.

Unexpressed anger doesn't go away. It may lead to a variety of problems, including unexplained attacks of panic, rage, or depression. Some of us have been angry since we were children and haven't felt safe to express it. It may be time to do so.

4. Grieve your losses. Grieving is one of the longest parts of the journey. You may simply have not gotten the love and nurture you needed. This is a sad thing and can't be overlooked. Like anger, sadness will not go away, but it can be hidden. Have you known people who get depressed or physically sick after they lose a significant loved one. Studies on grief have demonstrated that those who don't express their feelings of loss are extremely vulnerable. Simply having safe places to talk about loss is a great therapy.

5. Accept the truth about yourself. This simply means believing you are "fearfully and wonderfully" made and didn't deserve the harm that happened to you. You may have difficulties believing that. You may need others in your life who are able to speak the truth to you and be affirming.

6. Establish new boundaries. We have discussed how boundaries were violated in ways that cause harm. You probably didn't learn what healthy boundaries are and have no idea how to establish them for yourself. This is also an example of how you may need others to teach you and help you enforce boundaries.

7. Find meaning in your pain. Physical pain is similar to emotional and spiritual pain. It can guide us to what we need to do differently. It can push us to have more courage. Or it can take us out of our own pride and help us depend more on God. Certainly, our pain lets us identify with the pain of humanity and challenges us to be more compassionate. James, the brother of Christ, says, "Consider it pure joy, my brothers, whenever you face trials of many kinds, because you know that the testing of your faith develops perseverance. Perseverance must finish its work so that you may be mature and complete, not lacking anything" (James 1:2-4).

8. **Forgive those who hurt you.** Many of our clients get stuck in the healing process because they don't think about forgiving those who hurt them. Many people stay angry so they won't get hurt again. Some Christians are too quick, on the other hand, to forgive. There is a balance. We must not forget to forgive. We might even need to act as if we have forgiven someone before we will feel we have.

> **Some days we will have to decide we must talk about our feelings, get support, and forgive all over again.**

The great woman of faith Corrie ten Boom saw her sister die in a Nazi concentration camp. Years later she spoke at a gathering and recognized one of the cruelest camp guards in the audience. She felt that God was telling her to forgive this man. Against everything her mind was telling her, she forced herself to shake his hand and tell him that she forgave him. She felt this experience was tremendously freeing.

Healing in these ways is a lifelong journey. Some days we will have to decide we must talk about our feelings, get support, and forgive all over again. This is the experience of life.

UNDERSTANDING YOUR FANTASIES

We all have fantasies. They don't have to be sexual or romantic in nature. Some of us, for example, have sports fantasies—sinking the last shot, hitting the home run, or winning a tournament. Some of us identify with sports teams and fantasize that we are a part of it somehow. What are these fantasies doing? For some people, they might heal the wounds of past athletic failures.

Some of us have monetary fantasies. We imagine what it would be like to win the lottery. What would we do with all that money? We might fantasize about things like cars, boats, or houses. These fantasies may correct our insecurities about not having money, in the past or present. They might also portray to us that if we have money or possessions, others will like us. Some of us have even thought we might get more sex if we have lots of things. For instance, men may feel if they had fantasy cars, they would attract women.

Fantasies are attempts to heal wounds. They correct our self-perceptions and bring to us different results. They make us feel loved, accepted, affirmed, and cherished. Apply this principle to sexual or romantic fantasies. They could be healing our feelings of being unloved or unlovable. They bring us thoughts of touch and excitement. They bring us thoughts of love and romance. Sexual and romantic fantasies might also be the way we replay old situations, expecting different results or changing the roles. In our fantasies instead of being victims, we might be the ones in charge.

Another principle about fantasies is that many of the people or events in them can be symbolic. Imagined people can represent actual people in our past or current life. Certain behaviors can symbolize having control or power. Fantasies are powerful. They can even change brain chemistry and mood. If we are fantasizing about the excitement of romance or sexual conquest, the adrenalin of these thoughts can raise our moods. If we are fantasizing about the nurture of love and romance, powerful chemicals in our brains can sooth us and quiet our anxieties.

Therefore, you should understand what you fantasize about. Take a minute and see if you can quiet your spirit. Ask yourself, "What have been my sexual and romantic fantasies? Which ones have I replayed the most?" Ask yourself these four groups of questions:

1. In your most common fantasies who shows up? What do they look like? What other physical characteristics do they have that make them particularly romantically or sexually attractive to you?

2. Who shows up and what do they act like? Do they smile or frown? Are they kind? What do their eyes tell you? What do they say? How do they treat you?

3. Where does your most common fantasy take place? What is the setting and ambiance? Is it inside or outside?

4. What happens in your fantasies? What is the nature of sexual or romantic activity?

You may find that one group of these questions is the most significant. You may not care about what the people look like in your fantasies, as long as they are always nice. You may not care about sexual activity as long as the other person looks a certain way. You may only care about where it takes place. You may only be concerned about what activity happens.

What is your most common fantasy? For some of you it may help to remember the most common forms of pornography you use. For others it might help to remember what fantasies you use to masturbate or excite yourself during sex with your spouse.

If you find that doing this exercise has stimulated you in lustful ways, call someone and talk about how you feel. Then see if you can apply these principles to interpret your fantasies:

1. Who shows up may *look* like the person who most deeply abandoned you.

2. Who shows up may *look* or *act* in ways that you think brings comfort and or nurture to you. They may be the "magic" person who will correct all your needs for love.

3. There may be symbolic physical characteristics about the people who show up. A smile will suggest warmth. Certain hair colors suggest certain qualities that might be important to you.

> **No sexual thought or activity is so perverse that God can't forgive.**

4. Where it happens may also symbolize a variety of things. It could directly represent a scene from your past in which you felt safe. It could represent a place that you imagine will bring you comfort. It could be a place that represents excitement or passion. It could also represent a place where harm occurred, only in your fantasy the result is different or you are in control.

5. What happens can also be from direct memories of the past or of imagined situations. You may fantasize about things that happened to you because they produced comfort or excitement. You may imagine a different result. Remember that all sexual activities may symbolize certain qualities.

Some fantasies are about anger. Thinking about harming someone else may represent an old anger you have against someone.

Be gentle with yourself. Remember that no sin separates you from the love of God (Rom. 8:31-39). No sexual thought or activity is so perverse that God can't forgive. Talk to someone about what you are discovering. Ask him or her to help you discern what your fantasies are saying. Your fantasies are a window into your soul.

If we understand fantasies and give them voice, and if we find the love and nurturing that we need in healthy ways, fantasies may disappear.

Healing requires that we find safe places and safe people. When we find both of these, we've really found safe community. Community is essential to our healing from emotional pain. Community provides us with the possibility of having healthy relationships with our spouses and others. Relationships are so important to the healing journey that we will take the next two chapters to talk about them.

8

The Relational Dimension

Part One

The relational dimension addresses our basic need for community with others. It includes the relationship of husband and wife, as well as friendships. Since loneliness is a main factor in sexual sin, healthy relationships are a vital antidote. The lack of intimacy in the most important relationships contributes to sexual vulnerability.

Too often the words "intimacy" and "sex" are used interchangeably. This book is about sexually sinful behavior as a substitute for intimacy. Pastors sometimes have a lot of acquaintances but very few intimate friends. Clergy may have very little intimacy in their lives for various reasons such as family-of-origin issues, an attempt to avoid relationships with members of their congregations, or an "intimacy disability" in their own lives.

For many of us, being truly intimate is one of our greatest challenges. The road to intimacy is filled with paradoxes. For example, sometimes good relationships occasionally feel bad and unhealthy relationships feel terrific. We want to be close but also need distance. We long to 'be ourselves' with people but feel compelled to protect ourselves by concealing certain aspects of who we really are.

Probably each of us could come up with examples of this dilemma. In Dr. Earle's earlier days as a sex therapist he was naive about the power for potential pain in people's lives through pornography. As he has listened to pastors' stories, he has clearly seen the enormous power of pornography in many clergy lives. We long for people with whom we can have close relationships, but frequently run from potential intimacy because of our own fears.

Intimacy requires hard work. It involves mutual caring and the sharing of our innermost thoughts and feelings. It requires that we become vulnerable to the possibility of being hurt by another person. It requires us to be willing to say that we need others. We face possible perils at every turn. We're afraid we might have to change our lifestyles, have less control over our lives, have to give up independence, be hurt again or hurt someone else. We're afraid someone might find out that we are less impressive than we want to be considered. We face a risk of becoming so attached to someone that we will be devastated if that person leaves.

> **The fear of true intimacy frequently makes pornography seem very appealing.**

Pornography is seductive because it does not require direct contact with a human being. It is something we think we can control. We can open it or close it, turn on the computer or turn it off. Thus, the fear of true intimacy frequently makes pornography seem very appealing.

Here are eight qualities of true intimacy:
1. Trust
2. Self-worth
3. Positive regard for others
4. Interdependence
5. Tolerance for conflict, ambiguity, and imperfection
6. Self-disclosure
7. Courage
8. Intimacy role model[1]

These qualities are very hard for many of us to achieve. Pornography offers a quick escape with no relational demands. Many times pastors are burned out on interactions with people. It is certainly possible to be functional without being intimate. Intimacy is an art, and few of us are willing to become artists.

Unfortunately, intimacy is never a finished achievement but must be nurtured throughout a relationship. It would be wonderful if our seminaries provided adequate training for intimacy.

Pornography creates sexual isolation. Intimacy is about revealing yourself emotionally to another. Manipulation and intimacy do not go together. Intimacy is never about finding pleasuring by looking at another person or fantasizing outside of a healthy relationship. One major challenge with pornography is that its desire leads us away from intimacy to what becomes a need for new types of experiences.

Too frequently a person starts with what he or she describes as soft porn and discovers that this becomes boring. The brain becomes tolerant, as we described earlier. Few pastors can successfully maintain boundaries in using pornography. As they increasingly isolate themselves for this, they're less likely to find intimacy in their main relationships. When a pastor is using pornography, he or she is completely self-focused. This person has no room for giving to others.

All of us need others. We can meet that need in constructive ways or very destructive ways. When you come from a family in which members showed little emotion or affection and you meet someone who expresses feelings fairly easily, you may be tempted to equate intimacy with any demonstration of emotion. Dr. Patrick J. Carnes states, "But if the feelings are about high drama, betrayal and passionate reconciliations, it is not *intimacy*. It is *intensity*. And it is both absorbing and addictive."[2]

Confusing intimacy with an addictive relationship is tempting. Probably at one time or another, most of us have confused an addictive relationship with intimacy. Even in marriage it is possible to confuse the neurotic interactions with the healthy components. In her book *Is It Love or Is It Addiction?* Brenda Schaeffer states, "Real love can actually be experienced or felt as emanating from the heart. Many spiritual schools emphasize how the heart is the bridge between our human experience and our spiritual experience."[3]

Few pastors describe their porn habits as spiritual experiences. On the other hand, pastors often describe affairs as spiritual relationships. Sometimes to justify their behaviors in religious terms, pastors rationalize. Most clergy and their spouses will say their marriages are in a rut. Most of us realize the tremendous demands placed on clergy marriages. Having and maintaining intimacy is an enormous task.

One seductive aspect of pornography is that it is readily available, especially with the availability of Internet pornography. Internet relationships are not intimate. However, the Internet allows for a quick fix without the challenges of initiating or maintaining intimacy. Cybersex provides an opportunity not found in prostitution, since no other human being has to be directly involved. It is possible to have many sexual relationships by participating in different chat rooms.

Dr. Patrick Carnes says, "Perhaps no other medium serves the need for anonymous sex better than the Internet. It provides the ultimate in anonymity. Frequently, part of the attraction for these people is the risk of unknown persons and situations. People go on-line for the sole purpose of finding someone they do not know to be a sex partner. By definition, anonymous sex is not about being in a relationship. With anonymous sex, you do not have to attract, seduce, trick, or even pay. It is simply sex."[4]

So it is not surprising that the Internet currently provides the biggest challenge in pornography for pastors and others. The availability of material to fit the sexual habits of any pastor, combined with its affordability and anonymity, results in a highly lethal possibility.

Sometimes a clergy person fosters the idea that "I deserve this since I spend so much time serving the Lord and others." It is amazing how innovative we can be when it comes to rationalizing behavior that is antithetical to our faith and value system.

Richard said he believed he was not doing anything wrong when he watched Internet pornography in the middle of the night, because it was not taking time away from his work or family. So for more than three years he had been going on-line for sex at least twice a week. He discovered that one of these times for Internet sex occurred on Saturday night before he would preach on Sunday. Using pornography became almost a ritual for him. Needless to say, he did not tell *anyone* he had added this dynamic to his sermon preparation. This behavior abruptly ended when his wife, Pam, walked into his home office and saw him viewing pornography. They worked on their marriage, and he established a contract to never turn to Internet pornography again.

However, Richard and Pam realized the power of pornography later when he returned to the Net for his fix. Pam discovered his relapse when she was using his computer. This discovery led to more intensive therapy and to no further relapses.

Many married pornography users say being involved with pornography is not the same as cheating on a spouse. But they eventually realize that using pornography is similar to having an affair, since it means going outside of the marital relationship for sexual pleasure.

We have previously discussed the influence of childhood experiences in increasing vulnerability to pornography. Internet pornography gives us the opportunity to detach from traumatic experiences, much as children do through fantasy and emotionally detaching. So when the pastor is frustrated with his or her spouse, kids, or ministry challenges, cybersex is a "friend" who is always available. Because of the anonymity, it appears to be "safe sex."

The Internet provides an ability to interact with others while keeping a barrier between the pastor and other people. Dr. Carnes states:

> Cybersex provides the ultimate pseudo-connection with another person, the perfect impersonal personal relationship, with no hassles or demands or connection. Cybersex enables users to truly objectify the person on the other side of that computer connection. In real time, you are still forced to confront, at some level, the fact that you are interacting with a human being. He or she is there in front of you, moving, breathing, talking, and so on. On the Internet, nothing is really there, save a flickering image on a computer monitor.[5]

The click of a mouse can immediately end this involvement, unlike a marital relationship.

The growth of cybersex is phenomenal.

- As of January 1999, 19,542,710 different people per month visited the top-five pay-porn web sites, with 98,527,275 different people visiting the top-five free-porn web sites each month.
- In November 1999, Nielsen Net Ratings figures showed 12.5 million surfers visited porn sites in September from their homes, a 140 percent rise in traffic in just six months.
- More than 100,000 web sites are dedicated to selling sex in some way, not including chat rooms, E-mails, or other avenues for sexual contact on the Web.
- About 200 sex-related web sites are added each day.

An "intimacy résumé" can be a helpful tool, stating what you have to offer a partner in an intimate relationship.

- Sex trade is the third-largest economic sector on the Internet (software and computers rank first and second), generating $1 billion dollars annually.[6]

These statistics indicate how intoxicating cybersex is for many people, unfortunately including many clergy. A clergy person who regularly uses cybersex generally feels that its power is stronger than his or her power to stop the behavior. The habit is also empowered by isolation. A pastor may often seek isolation because of his or her personality type, stressors at home, or stressors at work. Internet pornography offers a way to avoid the demands of people in the pastor's life. When the pastor feels others are demanding too much, cybersex provides a drug for escape.

One pastor first checked out Internet pornography, saying he was just curious after some church members had confessed to using it. His curious miniresearch project turned into a chronic pattern as he began to use pornography daily. He was shocked at himself that this had occurred. One challenge was the easy accessibility of the material. His wake-up call came when a computer expert in the church volunteered to help him with computer problems and discovered the list of regular-accessed porn web sites on his pastor's computer. The pastor quickly entered therapy.

Since intimacy and pornography are antithetical, we must learn how to become more able to develop intimacy with others. It's helpful to write an "intimacy résumé," which includes what you have to offer a partner in an intimate relationship. The résumé can include your physical attributes, anything you do well, every personal, positive attribute that comes to your mind. List anything you enjoy doing, the main topics you could comfortably discuss, and the many things you wouldn't mind encouraging others to talk about so you could learn more. Summarize your previous experiences that qualify you as an intimate partner.

It would certainly be rare for such an audit to occur while a person is using cybersex. Internet sex increases the challenges of finding intimacy with God, self, and people who are special in our lives.

Another exercise is to list the ways you are intimacy disabled and intimacy able. Intimacy disabilities include our weaknesses when it comes to providing an intimate relationship for ourselves or others. Through the "intimacy able" category we can brag on ourselves about our strengths in this area. No matter how hooked we can be on pornography, all of us have strengths and weaknesses in pursuing intimacy. Take time to analyze your intimacy skills below:

Intimacy Disabled	Intimacy Able
1.	1.
2.	2.
3.	3.
4.	4.
5.	5.

The Bible consistently presents God as encouraging us to be intimate with Him and others. Jesus' life and ministry also suggests that regard for self and others is central to the Christian life. It would be wonderful if a commitment to Christ and to His work automatically helped us be intimate on a regular basis. Although loving relationships may be frightening for us, building them is a necessary part of recovery. We cannot recover from sexual sin in isolation. Many pastors have attempted to live the "straight and narrow" by isolation or "white knuckling." The rewards for successfully becoming more intimacy able are enormous.

> **The rewards for successfully becoming more intimacy able are enormous.**

Sex and intimacy have always been problematic for the church. Unfortunately, people in our churches have at least as much of a problem with cybersex as those in the population at large. However, few congregations will tackle this subject. Understandably it is one of the most frightening areas of self-disclosure for a pastor. Most of the time, we would rather crucify the person who becomes honest in this area than to be part of a redeeming, reconciling community.

Sadly, pastors sometimes have to go outside the Christian community for help. Clearly it makes no sense for a pastor to confess sexual challenges if the response will be like that of a lynch mob. Religious systems need to evaluate their responses to intimacy disability within churches and in the larger ecclesiastical world. No faith can afford to neglect the assiduous self-criticism of such an evaluation. In this regard, all of us who care about religious integrity are in the same boat. Certainly the ministry cannot be the one profession in which impaired professionals cannot function again after sustained recovery and continued "relapse prevention."

> **The more painful the topic of communication, the more essential it is to improve communication.**

The Olsons state, "The most important area distinguishing happy and unhappy couples is *communication*."[7] Certainly intimacy requires the maintenance of positive communication. When a pastor has used Internet pornography, communication patterns become very important in the self-disclosure dealing with sexual sin. Fortunately tools are available to help us to learn to communicate more effectively, such as the "Awareness Wheel" and "Listening Cycle" provided by Interpersonal Communication Programs.[8]

The more painful the topic of communication, the more essential it is to improve communication. It is sobering to listen to a pastor tell his wife that he's been using pornography. Nancy has been married to a pastor, John, for more than 30 years. As far she knew, he had never been unfaithful to her sexually. John says he had never used pornography or had an extramarital affair through 25 years of marriage. Then he was introduced to pornography over the Net while playing computer games. When he was spending 8 to 10 hours each week on the computer, Nancy became concerned about his time management and unavailability to the family. Then she learned he spent most of his time on the computer visiting pornographic sites. She became angry and asked him to leave the home. The couple went through a very painful time as he began to do therapy and attend 12-Step groups, including Sex Addicts Anonymous (SAA). She found help at a Codependents of Sex Addicts (COSA) group. They also found help as a couple at a Recovering Couples Anonymous (RCA) group.

This couple stated that they felt much safer at these 12-Step groups than they had ever felt in any sharing experience. An interesting but not unusual dynamic is that both of them said that their relationship to God immensely improved as they used a 12-Step workbook, attended individual and couples therapy, and did 12-Step work. At first, neither wanted to attend a "secular" group experience. However, they both discovered a freedom from image management and safety. They found a level of intimacy in their communication, which was very new in their marriage.

One tool helpful for working with the challenges of Internet pornography is the "Circles of Intimacy," developed by Marilyn Murray, which helps couples, individuals, and families begin healing. Needless to say, most of us as pastors would preach and teach that the following approach is biblical. However, the challenges in "walking" that "talk" lead to many transgressions. The Circles of Intimacy can help all of us to have a framework for healthier relationships with self, God, family, and others. There is no place for pornography in the Circles of Intimacy. Look to this way of auditing your personal life by filling in the information in the diagrams and sharing your awarenesses with at least one other person in your life.

CIRCLES OF INTIMACY, OF RESPONSIBILITY, OF IMPACT

Circle No.:

1. God and you

If you only have yourself in your No. 1 circle, you will be narcissistic and selfish.

If you only have God in your No. 1 circle, you are apt to be a martyr; your physical and emotional health will be damaged. Only *you* can keep you healthy.

If you have anyone or anything besides God and you in your No. 1 circle, it will cause you dysfunction—intellectually, emotionally, physically, spiritually, and in your relationships.

You can be intimate with someone else, even God, only to the degree with which you are intimate with, and know and understand, yourself.

2. Parents and siblings (if you are a child)

or

2a. Spouse or significant other (if you are an adult)

2b. Minor children (living at home)

You will experience pain
- when anyone leaves your No. 2 circle;
- when you have someone in your No. 2 circle and they do not have you in theirs, or vice versa;
- when you have more than one adult in the No. 2 circle. (Spouse *and* a parent or lover or adult child or some other.)

3. Older children, minor children (not living at home), grandchildren, close family and friends with whom you can share intimately

Many persons have many friends and acquaintances but do not feel free to share confidences and feelings with them. Men often do not have any friends in their No. 3 circles. They may have buddies for hunting, fishing, sports events, or work, but not share intimately with them. These men often expect their spouses to fill both their No. 2 and No. 3 circles.

4. and 5. Family, friends, work colleagues, etc.

Frequency of contact also determines the circle of these persons. The circles may fluctuate often, especially if you move or travel frequently.

Addictions, jobs, activities, pets, and so on, also can be in your circles. Your *responsibility* to others is directly related to their positions in your circles. To determine a person's or thing's position in your circles, consider the person's or thing's *impact* upon you. The ability to cause you joy or pain is what determines the nearness of someone or something to the center of the circles.

HOW TO DETERMINE WHO IS IN YOUR NO. 2 AND NO. 3 CIRCLES

1. Is this a *safe* relationship?
2. Am I willing to be vulnerable with him or her?
3. Do I trust him or her?
4. Is he or she honest with me?
5. Is the relationship one sided?
6. Is there mutual sharing?
7. Is there mutual respect?
8. Is there mutual nurturing?
9. Is the relationship mutually rewarding?

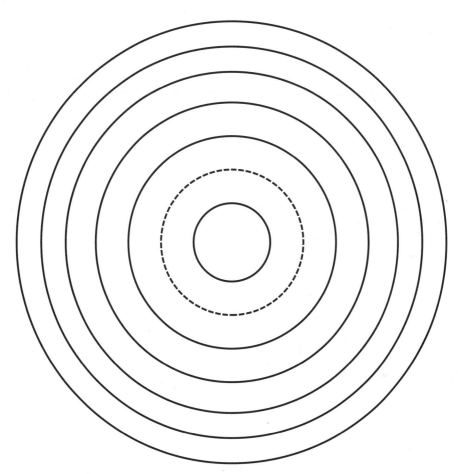

CIRCLES OF INTIMACY, RESPONSIBILITY, AND IMPACT

10. Do I enjoy being with him or her?
11. Is he or she glad to be with me?
12. Does he or she act pleased when he or she sees me?
13. Can I be my "original feeling child" with him or her?
14. Does he or she encourage and bring out my "original feeling child"?
15. Am I comfortable/relaxed with him or her, or am I uptight and anxious?
16. Do we find each other interesting?
17. What is my "history" with him or her? Have we shared happy, sad, and/or interesting times together over a long period of time?

18. What are our shared interests?
19. Do we have shared values?
20. What is our frequency of contact?

Throughout this book, we suggest homework assignments. The Circles of Intimacy can help us practice what we preach. Certainly nothing is new in this way of looking at intimacy. However, most of us have huge gulfs between our belief systems, intentions, and actions.

When we treat pastors, we find that they rarely put God, self, and spouse before work. This challenge is not unique to pastors. However, something about doing the "Lord's work" seduces them to get their lives out of balance. Pastors' kids frequently tell of an absent father or mother during childhood. It is sad that most of us face these challenges when we are "working in the trenches."

Unfortunately, many pastors tell us they have no one to talk to about painful feelings in their lives, especially in relationship to a topic such as Internet pornography. Pastors often tell us in therapy that this is the first time they have ever talked to anyone about their double lives.

> **Any of us can break relationship ruts in a number of ways, including appropriate humor.**

Most pastors counsel couples and know that couples notoriously get into ruts in their relationships. As we know, being in a rut is antithetical to intimacy. Most pastors and their spouses do not address the need for change until something significant forces them to make changes. The discovery of Internet pornography is one such crisis and requires major emotional surgery in the lives of the pastor and spouse.

Mike and Joan came in for therapy when Mike's use of pornography was discovered. Both stated their relationship was in a rut and felt bored in the relationship and with each other. I told them I guessed they were right, because I thought they were boring. Before saying that, I'd prayed, asking God to help me make sense. The couple immediately dropped their boring air and became angry with me. When that dynamic was processed, we had a good laugh.

Any of us can break relationship ruts in a number of ways, including appropriate humor. Laughing at themselves is sometimes an inexpensive, ready healing experience in a couple's relationship. Prov. 17:22 even tells us that laughing promotes good health: "A cheerful heart is good medicine, but a crushed spirit dries up the bones." Laughing and playing with your marital partner is a healthy way to enrich the relationship.

Another homework assignment we frequently give couples is to have both partners let themselves play. We ask couples to play games such as having water gun fights, throwing water balloons, playing hide-and-seek, or doing something to break the monotony of their relationships. Even when couples are pretty good about playing with young children, parents themselves seldom just have fun together. It is too easy to get into the rut of being too serious.

Another possibility is for a couple to take turns planning dates, with each partner trying to do something both can enjoy, always considering what the other partner would like to do.

When a husband and wife come to therapy because of Internet pornography, the first priority is probably not to go out and have fun together while they're experiencing incredible feelings of betrayal and anger. So they first need to deal with the pain in the relationship. The good news about the brokenness caused by sexual sin in the relationship is that the couple can develop a deeper intimacy than they had before.

A common problem for ministry couples is when most or all of their social times together are church activities. This almost always blocks intimacy.

Dr. Carnes suggests a helpful step for a couple in a relationship destroyed by pornography: "Overcome sexual shame through affirmation of each other. Couples that did the best emphasized the strategy of mutual affirmation. Compliment your partner. Affirm all the positive things you can see about his or her sexuality and about your sexuality together. Don't stop."[9]

We regularly encourage pastoral couples to look into each other's eyes and tell each other what they like about the other person without any qualification or "yes, but." No matter how much frustration, hurt, anger, or shame, we believe it is important to break through the pain in the crisis and affirm each other's positive aspects. Intimacy is not easily sustained. However, it is possible to re-create or create for the first time a depth of intimacy in a couple's relationship no matter how much frustration they have experienced.

In the next chapter we will look more specifically at restoring marriages that have been damaged by sexual sin. Trust can be established, and new and more passionate levels of intimacy can be created. Read on, there is hope.

9

The Relational Dimension

Part Two

In this chapter we want to speak specifically to those who would like to repair relationships that have been damaged by sexual sin or addiction. We know that repairing and rebuilding these relationships is one of the most difficult things there is. We also know this is one of the most rewarding journeys. We have worked with hundreds of couples who have developed more intimate relationships.

One word the Christian community often uses to refer to this process is "restoration." Marriages damaged by infidelity can be *restored*. We restore our marriages to fidelity, a return to the sacredness of the marriage vows.

The word "restore," however, should not connote "going back" to some place where everything was "right" with the marriage such as "the early years." Debbie and Mark Laaser, for example, often heard, "Just go back to the love you had when you were dating."

Such advice completely misses the process over time of building intimacy in marriage. It assumes that everything was good at one point and somehow got off track.

Going back historically really means going back to the same level of loneliness. Remember, we don't blame sexual sin on marital dysfunction. No level of marital distance warrants sexual sin. Usually both partners in such a marriage have been lonely and may have brought their own emotional and spiritual issues to the altar. They probably didn't know about these issues—the process of being married uncovered them. The task of restoration, really, is to learn how to heal these issues and how to build intimacy with God and with each other.

One of our assumptions about marriages that have experienced infidelity is that they began with two wounded people who found each other. Mark Laaser and his wife, along with Pat Carnes, call this the quality of "heat seeking missiles." In chapter 7 we described the various trauma reactions people can have. One, the "trauma bond," occurs when two wounded people find each other hoping to work out their wounds with each other. Each one must play a part and have a similar agenda. Much of this is unconscious.

When Pat stood at the altar ready to marry Shirley, for example, he didn't remember that he was sexually abused by his dad when he was very small. Pat was also not aware that his mother had not nurtured him emotionally or spiritually. Pat's mom was not a bad mother, just distant and insecure. Throughout his life he had turned to pornography and masturbation for comfort. Now as he faced his bride, he hoped she would be the answer to all of his loneliness and neediness. As he went off to the honeymoon, he also hoped marital sex would eliminate his sexual temptations.

> **Sexual sin is painful and wounds the spouse.**

Carnes studied sex addicts and spouses for his book, *Don't Call It Love*. He found that 81 percent of all sex addicts are sexual-abuse survivors, 74 percent are physical-abuse survivors, and 97 percent are emotional-abuse survivors. Amazingly, he found that the abuse statistics for spouses was identical.[1] This study suggests that pastors who are sexually addicted have married people who are equally wounded. Two wounded people, if you consider the common abuse statistics, will have a difficult time creating healthy sexuality.

We believe the only way to heal a relationship suffering from such wounds is for both husband and wife to work equally hard at healing them. This may be difficult in the early days of discovery for couples facing sexual sin. Sexual sin is painful and wounds the spouse. It may trigger the spouse into memories of past harm that he or she may not even be aware of. This can be like a double dose of harm—the pain of old wounds is multiplied with the pain of the new wounds. No wonder so many spouses have such difficult times.

In the early days after the discovery of sexual sin, it is critical for both spouses to get support. Unfortunately, the wounded spouse has a harder time finding this support. Many pastors' spouses even get blamed for the sexual sins of their partners. Many people have the inaccurate notion that if the spouse had been more sexually available, the pastor might not have done what he or she did. This thinking reflects how difficult it is for many to accept that a pastor is anything but perfect (so it must be someone else's fault).

Many spouses tell horror stories of how even church hierarchies have told them to "forgive and forget" and to be more sexually available and things will be all right. Beth, for example, had just learned that her husband was caught downloading pornography on the church computer. She was devastated. She was in a state of shock and trying to keep things together for the kids. She was too embarrassed to talk to any other women. One night several weeks later, several of the male elders from the church showed up at her door. They had a bag from a lingerie store and told her that if she would use what was inside, everything would be all right.[2]

Stories like this remind us that the spouse will need a lot of support from people who understand the devastation of the problem. Only later, when some state of "normal" has returned, might the spouse be able to look at his or her own issues. Mark Laaser's spouse, Deb, has lived through this journey and emphasizes that it is critical for the spouse to seek support and counseling—not just to survive but to grow.

If both spouses are wounded, they need to learn to hear and accept each other's pain. This may be very difficult for the wounded spouse in the early days. He or she will not want to hear any "excuse" for the sexual sin. Since it will also be hard for them to look at their own pain, mutual sharing may take a while to develop.

We have found that this dynamic often leads therapists to recommend that the couple not talk to each other for a time. It is also a common recommendation that they do only individual counseling and not come together. It may also be true that therapists recommend that they separate for a time to heal.

We understand the need for individual counseling and for boundaries in what couples talk about. But right away, couples need counseling to know how much to talk, what to expect, and what to tell the kids and others and to even begin the process of mutual understanding. It may be necessary to live separately if a potential abuse problem exists. It is much harder to know how to live under the same roof with appropriate boundaries and space. The wounded spouse, for example, may not feel like having any contact with his or her partner, and these concerns should be considered carefully.

We believe the process of healing can proceed if the couple is involved in three main avenues of healing work. The husband and wife each will need counseling and support (the first two avenues). The couple will need equal counseling and support for their relationship (the third avenue). Recovering Couples Anonymous (RCA) symbolizes this with a three-legged stool. Without any of the three legs, the stool will fall.

In chapter 7 we said one aspect of healing from trauma was that a person needs a "fair witness." This means someone who hears and knows about the pain. It is obviously important that if a couple survives, both spouses become fair witnesses to each other. This will mean they need a safe place where they can hear each other's stories as each one begins to understand. Effective counseling in the early days will include places where this can happen.

> **When a couple hears each other's pain, the pain stops just being "my" pain and becomes "our" pain.**

We have found that even if the couple think they know each other, they really don't. How could they when the information that needs to be shared is only being discovered for the first time? This can be a long, painful journey, but we have seen how moving and healing it can be for two people to really get to know each other for the first time.

When a couple hears each other's pain, the pain stops just being "my" pain and becomes "our" pain. For example, if one spouse has been sexually abused as a child, the abuse also happened to the other spouse because he or she will be affected by it in marriage. The pain of the one who was sexually abused is indirectly the pain of the one he or she marries. Understanding this is a vital move. The couple that can begin to accomplish this will be light years ahead of most couples in intimacy.

Couples who seek to heal will need to learn how to be more intimate, as we discussed in the last chapter. We believe so strongly in this that we are providing you with another way of looking at intimacy. It is a way for you to rate both yourself and your spouse (and for your spouse to do the same, if you are both courageous) as to how intimacy able you and your partner are as a couple.[3]

In this exercise the concept of intimacy has been broken into seven components. On the Intimacy Dimensions chart you will find in the left column qualities of healthy intimacy, while in the right column are qualities of unhealthy intimacy.

In the "Initiative" category, for example, a person who can be intimate in a healthy way will be able to reach out to others; risk expressions of caring (to say, "I love you" or "I missed you"); invite others to share activities; talk about problems with others; and express desires and needs to another. Those who have problems with intimacy are passive and isolated, unable to ask for what they need, assume the role of victim (they feel they have little or no power), and often feel as if no one cares for them.

INTIMACY DIMENSIONS[4]

Healthy Intimacy

Unhealthy Intimacy

Initiative

One of the characteristics of healthy intimacy is the ability to begin a relationship or reach out to others. This involves taking the risk to express how much you care for the person, how you want his or her time and attention, and how much you are attracted to the person (emotionally, spiritually, or physically). Initiative also includes the ability to invite a person to share in activities and a willingness to share your own problems and issues.

The inability to reach out and begin a relationship characterizes intimacy dysfunction. Instead, you stay passive and detached. At times you may assume a victim posture and blame others for bad things happening to you. You may also have the feeling that you have been abandoned and you are helpless to do anything about it.

Presence

The ability to meet others, to listen, and to attend to another's thoughts and feelings marks healthy intimacy. You can share your own reactions. You can reveal feelings honestly. The person you are with knows you genuinely are present in the relationship.

With intimacy dysfunction, you do not make your feelings available. You isolate yourself. You do not accept attention and may divert attention away from yourself. Addictions and other dysfunctional behaviors keep you numb to feelings and turn others away.

Closure

Healthy intimacy involves the ability to finalize arrangements, complete transactions, end fights, and solve problems. You can respond to requests, desires, and attractions without getting lost in the other's identity. This includes the ability to accept help and to say "Thank you."

Without healthy intimacy skills, you tend to exaggerate problems instead of solving them, use excuses, and blame others for your problems. You may use chronic busyness and work overload as an excuse not to complete work. You hold issues open and avoid closure.

Vulnerability

Vulnerability is the ability to share what you are thinking or feeling. You can talk about yourself with others, including problems that you are facing. You can ask for help in problem solving.

In unhealthy intimacy you keep your thought process private, do not ask for help, and may have private conversations with yourself and debate back and forth about what to do.

Nurture

With healthy intimacy you can care for others with no expectation of something in return. You have empathy for and can support others. You make suggestions and do not feel rejected if they are not taken. You show physical affection (holding hands, giving hugs) without it having sexual meaning. You can express feedback in affirming and supportive ways.

Relationships built on unhealthy intimacy lack nurture. You take care of others in order to control them or get something in return. You build your self-esteem on your ability to give care. You cannot accept another person's feelings and make efforts to discount the other's feelings. Physical touch may have ulterior motives, like sex.

Honesty

Healthy intimacy involves the ability to be clear about what you believe and feel, express anger in positive ways, express either negative or positive feelings, and openly share disagreements or resentments.

Unhealthy intimacy is dishonest. You claim to not have deep feelings, disguise your anger to avoid making waves or conflict, use anger as a way of controlling another person, do not share your beliefs, attitudes, or values, may tell lies to gain approval, and avoid direct communication by using others to relay messages.

Play

People who have healthy skills see the humor in life and laugh easily. They put effort into nonwork activities and search for opportunities to play. They feel free to take risks and try new ventures, and they enjoy children. They exhibit the ability to smell the roses, enjoy a sunset, and engage in celebrations of God's creation. They are willing to play in noncompetitive ways and do not feel guilty just because they take time to play.

With unhealthy intimacy you may be compulsively busy and miss significant events. You take a grim, "Life is a problem," stance; refuse to try new things, take a risk, or go on an adventure; rarely laugh; express the belief that children should be seen and not heard; have few or no hobbies, unless in compulsive, competitive, or income producing ways; have no idea how to enjoy life with another person.

As you look at the Intimacy Rating Scales below, you'll notice that the scale on the left is for you, and the one on the right is for your spouse. To begin, look at the "Initiative" category in the Intimacy Dimensions chart. If you feel the descriptions of healthy intimacy in that category fit you perfectly, give yourself a 10. If you feel the unhealthy characteristics fit you perfectly, give yourself a 1. If you recognize that you have both healthy and unhealthy characteristics in this category, you will fall somewhere in between 1 and 10 on the scale. Rate your spouse in the same way.

Fill out the rest of the categories just as you have done this first one, rating both you and your spouse on each. When you finish, you will have a chart that shows an intimacy rating for both your spouse and yourself. When you and your spouse both have completed this exercise, exchange your chart with his or hers. Use this information to help discuss intimacy with each other.

INTIMACY RATING SCALES

You   Spouse

Low 1 2 3 4 5 6 7 8 9 10 High   Low 1 2 3 4 5 6 7 8 9 10 High

Initiative

1 ————————————10   1 ————————————10

Presence

1 ————————————10   1 ————————————10

Closure

1 ————————————10   1 ————————————10

Vulnerability

1 ————————————10   1 ————————————10

Nurture

1 ————————————10   1 ————————————10

Honesty

1 ————————————10   1 ————————————10

Play

1 ————————————10   1 ————————————10

Again, note where and how much your ratings agree or dis-agree with your spouse's. Discuss with each other the relative state of intimacy in your marriage. Don't be discouraged, because no marriage is perfect. This exercise is a road map, a place to start talking. The categories can also give you ideas about the qualities of healthy intimacy you may want to work on.

You may want to work on some of the dimensions of intimacy that are a problem for you. If so, clearly decide which ones you're going to work on, and on how you will address each issue. For example, perhaps you decide that in the intimacy category "Play," you want to learn how to golf with your spouse. First, determine what steps you will need to take to make this a greater part of your life. You might check in the phone book for places that teach golf, for example. You could look in the newspaper for golf courses near you. Remember that your reticence to golf may stem from embarrassing childhood experiences. Or it may relate to a core belief that you won't be able to golf well enough for your spouse and that he or she will leave you because of this. Share your feelings with your spouse as you become aware of them. This is another way to be courageous in your marriage and to take risks.

BUILDING TRUST

The intimacy exercise is just one example of the work that is necessary build new forms of communication in your marriage. There are many other ways to learn how to communicate about feelings, to learn how to play, to fight fairly, and to set healthy boundaries. Books, seminars, and ministries can help you do this. Realize that these resources help some aspects of restoration but perhaps not others. Hundreds of couples who come to us tried books, workshops, and seminars that didn't really help because the core wounds weren't addressed. Many of the Christian workshops, books, and seminars that exist are really for the couple that is basically doing well and wants to do better. A couple that has faced infidelity cannot escape the hard and painful work of healing deep wounds.

"But if we hope for what we do not yet have, we wait for it patiently" (Rom. 8:25).

In his workbook *Faithful and True,* Mark Laaser described seven keys to restoring trust in a relationship.[5]

Trust is

Christ Centered
Committed
Continuing
Communicating
Consistent
Considerate
Control Surrendered

Christ Centered

Being Christ centered means that trust reflects the sacred nature of relationship. The Bible tells us that a husband and wife become one flesh. However, this must not blur their individuality, since the marital bond is composed of the two persons as well as the relationship. Paul says the relationship between a man and woman is like the relationship between Christ and the Church (Eph. 5). Something about one flesh must have Christ in it.

Perhaps this means a husband and wife must have a Christlike attitude toward each other, an attitude of sacrifice. This includes a holiness and sacredness. A man and a woman are one flesh. They are a unity, a oneness. Have you heard your kids describe you as

> **There is a mystical and spiritual union that happens between a man and woman in marriage.**

"my parents." You are a collective unity in their minds. There is a mystical and spiritual union that happens between a man and woman in marriage. It is God ordained. Rebuilding trust begins with prayer between spouses that they again become a sacred union and that they celebrate Christ together.

Committed

Sometimes all of us must agree to something before we feel like doing it. When we seek to build trust, we may not feel trust, but we can be committed to try. Recognizing the Christ-centered nature of a relationship, we can want to trust. This is important. It signals to our spouses, family members, or friends that we will exert the emotional and spiritual effort to build trust. This will be an act of the mind and not the heart in the early weeks or months. At some points we must act as if we are committed and agree to steps necessary to work on relationship.

Continuing

Often when sexual sinners repent of sin, they want their spouses to trust them *right away*. They may even quote scriptures about forgiveness. Is this request really fair and reasonable? No. Damaged emotions and spirits may take time to heal. With God's help and lots of support and help, they will. This, however, is a *process* that occurs over time. For one thing, those of us who have damaged trust must recognize that our partners will be grieving a loss—the loss of their trust. Grieving occurs slowly.

When we teach our children to drive cars, and they start driving alone, we set some limits. Our kids may object and say, "Don't you trust me?" We are in a Christ-centered relationship with our children, and we seek to guide and protect them. We are committed to trusting them. They many never have done anything to damage our trust. Driving is a new experience, however, and building trust will be a process. They will earn our trust on an ongoing basis.

Communicating

Building trust demands that people in relationships communicate. Few things damage trust like feeling the other person isn't being honest. Make sure you have regular times to talk and that you have strategies in place for honestly expressing feelings. Remember the shame-based core belief that says, "No one will like me as I am." Some of us have operated by that belief, and it has caused us to hide facts about some past and present behaviors. Our partners can interpret these lies and omissions to mean that we really don't love them—otherwise we'd tell the truth.

Developing trust can mean that we tell our spouses, family members, and friends about our past—including the sinful behaviors. The thought of doing this can be *really* frightening. We are afraid of losing them. Ask yourself, "Do I really want to live the rest of my life wondering if my spouse (or family member or friend) finds __(your history)__ out about me, whether or not she (or he) will be repulsed and leave me."

Remember several things about truth telling:

1. Never tell the truth to punish someone else, for example: "If you were a better wife, I wouldn't have had to go out and have that affair. Now I'll tell you about it." This does not mean you should avoid telling the truth because the other person will be hurt. The key is *your* intention. If you are telling the truth to develop intimacy and build trust, then it can be healing.

2. Never tell the truth to manipulate forgiveness, for example: "I'll tell you the truth, the whole truth, and nothing but the truth. Now you need to forgive me, and we need to move on." This "forgive and forget" strategy is selfish and doesn't consider the other person's pain and need for healing time.

3. Hearing the truth about the past should never lead to the other person using that information to punish the teller. The hearer should also not assume that this knowledge will let him or her better watch for symptoms of future sinful behavior.

Consistent

Trust will be built when behavior is consistent over time. If you say you will stop a certain sinful behavior, you must be able to do that over time. In addictive behavior, this is called maintaining sobriety. If you pledge to do something, such as keep a marriage vow, you must be consistent in doing it over time. So often we have seen addicts quickly tell their spouses, "You can trust me now." That is rather naive. If lies, deceptions, and various inconsistent behaviors have been a

Behavior that is consistently repentant, humble, and corrected will eventually heal the wounds.

part of your past, how will you demonstrate that you are different. You must be able to do so over time.

Some marriages, for example, have been living with lies for years. It won't take years to restore trust, but it certainly won't take just a few days or weeks. Behavior that is consistently repentant, humble, and corrected will eventually heal the wounds. Consistency applies to all behaviors. If you say you'll be home for dinner at 6 P.M., be home at 6 P.M. Keep your promises. Do what you say you're going to do. If something comes up that prevents you from doing so, offer explanations that are not selfish excuses or blaming.

Considerate

If trust has been violated in your relationship by your sinful behaviors, you have damaged your partner. This means several things:

1. Don't expect the other person to heal overnight.
2. Expect current events to occasionally trigger past pain.
3. Be willing to listen to your partner's pain, no matter how old it is.

David had a number of affairs years ago. He confessed, repented, and has been faithful since then. Kathy has forgiven him, and David's consistent behavior has helped them build trust again. One day Kathy saw David talking to an attractive lady at church. Although the two were only discussing superficial things, Kathy was reminded of her past pain. She was hurt and angry and stormed out of church.

David has two response choices. He can get angry with Kathy and say, "Don't you trust me after all these years? You embarrassed me by storming out of church. What you saw was nothing."

David could find Kathy and say, "I can see that my talking with that woman must have looked bad. Can you tell me about your hurt? If you'd like, I'm willing to explain that nothing was going on with her."

Which response do you think builds better trust?

David must be willing to accept on an ongoing basis that one consequence of his sin is the damage done to Kathy. While he desperately wants her not to be hurt and is honestly embarrassed by her reaction, expressing his anger is not a good choice.

Being considerate of your spouse's, family members', or friend's needs and emotions will help you build trust.

Control Surrendered

Building trust is like being saved. We surrender our lives to Christ and give up control. We find joy, peace, and eternal life in return. Surrendering control of the actions of our spouses, family members, or friends is the same way. We can't control their behaviors, make them love us, or prevent them from sinning. They must be motivated to find love for us and freedom from sin on their own. We must be willing to lose our relationships in order to get them back. We must surrender our partners to God's care.

This applies to all relationships. Think of some times when you had to let go.

—Your child learned to walk; you let go of his or her hands.

—Your child went to school; you waved good-bye.

—Your child learned to drive; you gave him or her the keys.

—Your child got married; you gave him or her away.

Recall the joy and peace of being saved by Christ. Reaffirm your surrender to God, and surrender your relationships to Him as well.

We know finding trust is not as simple as following this basic outline. But rebuilding trust can happen over time. We have known many couples that have done so. Ultimately, trusting is an attitude. It is not based on some complete work of private detection by the one who has been offended by the sexual sin. It is not based on the offending spouse being in some form of prison and reporting in all the time. It is also not based on the administration of some kind of lie detector test. However, sometimes a polygraph may be used in clinical treatment either for detection and/or to help establish new trust. Trust is the ability to look someone in the eye who is humble and honest and know that he or she is telling the truth. Trust is letting go. It is giving the future to God's providence.

Many spouses we talk to tell us they really don't think much anymore about whether or not their husband or wife is being faithful. They have come to know a deeper intimacy. This gives them a sense of peace and assurance that they are in a faithful relationship. If their spouses ever became distant again, then they might worry. The key is to always stay connected emotionally and spiritually.

DEVELOPING A VISION

To all of you who struggle with infidelity, there is hope. Do you realize how many couples today struggle with sexual sin and brokenness? You are not alone if you struggle with these issues. We encourage you to find fellowship with others who can relate to your story. When we find fellowship with others who struggle, "our pain" becomes the pain shared by a community of people. As we experience that, we will realize that our pain is the pain of all humanity.

We will say more about this in our next chapter, but for now let us contend that couples who know how to "come back" from the experience of sexual brokenness and who find new levels of intimacy will use their pain to be more effective ministry partners.

> Couples who know how to "come back" from the experience of sexual brokenness and who find new levels of intimacy will use their pain to be more effective ministry partners.

Becoming ministry partners is challenging. As a husband and wife grow in spiritual maturity together, they will ask one key question, "What would God have us do together?"

Bob had been a minister who struggled with pornography and other sexual behaviors. He has been "sober" now for several years, and Ruth, his wife, has found her trust restored. The two of them have struggled with many deep emotional issues and know each other now better than ever before. Bob is about to be restored to a parish ministry. Ruth is a mother and a schoolteacher. As the time approaches for them to move to their new church, Ruth becomes angry about lots of little things and can't figure out why.

Ruth had been wounded by her husband's sexual sins. Because he had been a minister, the sexual sins had also impacted her faith. Her faith and trust in ministry is still damaged in many ways she doesn't even realize. As she faces returning to her role as a minister's wife, she is not quite sure she is ready. She would rather that Bob stay in his secular job where he is making more money anyway!

We have known many situations just like this. A spouse's trust is impaired in his or her role as ministry partner. Bob and Ruth never discussed Bob's return to ministry. Bob just assumed that this is what he was trained for and what he wanted to do again. He felt called by God and held on to Phil. 1:6, that God would be faithful to complete His work in him. Bob needed to be restored in his mind. It was a powerful symbol of God's and others' forgiveness.

The main problem is that Bob and Ruth had never talked about ministry. In fact, they never really prayed or studied scripture with each other. Each had a personal relationship with God, but they did not have one *together*. We believe that a ministry couple is called to find its calling as a couple. We use the word "vision" to suggest that all couples need a direction to follow. They need to know where they are going. To paraphrase the Bible, "A couple without a vision will perish" (see Prov. 29:18, KJV). The word "vision" appears in the Bible. Great leaders have vision. The great visions are of what God is going to do on earth and in people's lives.

Over time Ruth and Bob discussed ministry together. Bob said one very important thing to her, "We are a couple. My calling, I believe, is from God. I don't always trust myself or my ability to discern God's will. I would like it if you would also pray and pray with me. If you don't feel called as I do, then we need to find God's direction for our lives together." Bob gave Ruth the freedom to find God's will on her own. He didn't try to manipulate her or force the issue. Eventually, Ruth reclaimed her role as ministry spouse. Together they can build a vision of what kinds of ministry they might do together.

In the next chapter on the spiritual dimension of healthy sexuality, we want to understand more deeply how maturing spiritually is the ultimate answer to freedom from sexual temptations.

10

Spiritual Healing

Pastors and parishioners alike are often frustrated and ashamed that they still struggle with sexual lust and temptation. They've prayed to be healed, and God hasn't delivered them. As we've described, men and women who struggle with sex are depressed and shame filled to begin with. Their ongoing frustration contributes to these old feelings. Many become angry with God. Is He not the God they believe in, the One who answers prayer?

As pastors, we have discovered that our personal brokenness has led to a deeper understanding of what it means to really trust God, to turn our lives over to His will. This is the movement from head knowledge to heart knowledge. This may only happen through brokenness. We have found that many clergy we have worked with have discovered a deeper faith through God's grace manifested in forgiveness and healing. It is unfortunate that it sometimes takes a wake-up call, a "crash and burn," to help us experience the deeper meanings of biblical verses and theological beliefs.

In 2 Cor. 12:7-10, Paul writes this:

> To keep me from becoming conceited because of these surpassingly great revelations, there was given me a thorn in my flesh, a messenger of Satan, to torment me. Three times I pleaded with the Lord to take it away from me. But he said to me, "My grace is sufficient for you, for my power is made perfect in weakness." Therefore I will boast all the more gladly about my weaknesses, so that Christ's power may rest on me. That is why, for Christ's sake, I delight in weaknesses, in insults, in hardships, in persecutions, in difficulties. For when I am weak, then I am strong.

Spiritual maturity and healing from sexual lust and temptation begins with this last sentence of Paul's: "For when I am weak, then I am strong." Bill Wilson, cofounder of Alcoholics Anonymous, recognized this spiritual truth when he wrote the first step of AA: "I admitted that I was powerless over alcohol and that my life had become unmanageable."

We are never saved or healed through our own strength. This comes only through God's love and mercy. Recognizing our own weaknesses is the only way to let go of our need to control our own lives. It is the only way to let go of our pride and need to find approval. Often the humility from our brokenness allows us to truly know and trust God.

We have also found that acknowledging our own stories of brokenness is the way that we connect with others. In a recent workshop for women who struggle with sex addiction, a Roman Catholic nun was a participant. At age 65 she had struggled with sexual sin all of her life and had been sexual with at least 15 priests during her years of service to the Church. She was completely broken as she told us her story. After the workshop, the group of Catholics and Protestants from all different denominations shared Communion. Afterward, this nun told us, "That was the first time I felt I really experienced the body and blood of Christ."

Out of the depths of His death came the victory of the Resurrection.

That was quite a statement for one who comes from a religious tradition that believes only a priest can celebrate Communion. Strength did not create this experience. It was weakness. It was the fellowship of common sinners who experienced the body and blood of Christ.

We have recently tried to understand Jesus' words in Matt. 11:28-30: "Come to me, all you who are weary and burdened, and I will give you rest. Take my yoke upon you and learn from me, for I am gentle and humble in heart, and you will find rest for your souls. For my yoke is easy and my burden is light."

What could Jesus possibly mean by saying that we will find rest by taking on His burden? His burden, the salvation of the world, did not seem particularly light. His pain and suffering were not particularly comforting. In His humanity He experienced the pain of the world. In the Garden of Gethesemane He anguished over the pain of death. He experienced the loneliness of His disciples betraying Him and denying Him. On the Cross Jesus felt that

God had abandoned Him. Out of the depths of His death came the victory of the Resurrection.

To take on Jesus' burden is to understand that all of us experience the pain of loneliness, abandonment, and death. If we believe pain and loneliness are unique to us, we can get very depressed and angry. If we believe we are not alone, that even God in Christ understands that pain, the burden becomes much lighter. In another workshop a pastor revealed elements of his story to the group that he had never told anyone before. After sharing this, he said he felt as if a burden had been lifted from him. It was the burden of years of silence. The yoke was lighter. He found comfort in sharing.

Recovery from pornography and other sexual sins is for those who are spiritually and emotionally broken. It is for the weary, the burdened, the frightened, and the lonely. It is not for those who think they can do it alone. We all need God and each other. It is therefore imperative that a recovery program includes increasing our time of fellowship with God and with each other. At times we will seek to commune with God by ourselves, and at times we will seek to do so with others.

In chapter 1 we outlined the stage of sexual addiction in which a person pursues a ritual to sexually act out. This ritual can be creative and take hours per day. We believe if we would spend even a portion of that time on spiritual rituals, or disciplines, we would come closer to God.

In chapter 6 we discussed the role of fantasy in sexual sin. We believe that all fantasies are attempts to heal emotional and spiritual wounds. They are our ideas of the ways romantic and sexual encounters can substitute for real intimacy with God and each other. To combat fantasy, we must find ways to focus our minds on "unseen things above." One word we could use for this is "vision."

We discussed how couples need to develop a shared vision in the last chapter. We believe we all need a sense of purpose, calling, and direction in our lives. A vision is a mental picture of a preferable future. It is a picture of where God would have us go. It is a calling.

How many of you struggle to know what that is? Many of us have never known a sense of peace about our direction in life. Instead we stumble along reacting to things that happen to us. We might get mad at ourselves and at others because we never seem to "get anywhere." In the story *Alice and Wonderland,* Alice comes to a fork in the road. She asks, "What fork do I take?" She is asked, "Where are you going?" She responds, "I don't know." She is then told, "Then either path will take you there."

> **Those who have been broken through sexual sin can often find great opportunity.**

We have found that those who have been broken through sexual sin can often find great opportunity. They may be experiencing the pain of having been fired from various jobs and the possibility that they can't return to the same kind of work. This "crashing and burning" may give a freedom to really know God's will. All the categories of what they are supposed to do have melted down. They will now be free to really discern God's direction. They will have to grieve what has been lost. But they can also find great freedom in knowing there are other possibilities to pursue.

Earlier we referred to the story of the Jewish people in Num. 13 and 14. When they faced the prospect of going to the Promised Land, which they had never seen, they balked at the prospect of being "devoured" by the "giants" in the land (see 13:32-33, NIV, KJV). They wanted to return to Egypt and slavery. Their only vision of where they needed to go was a fearful one. Eventually, a man who had faith and a vision, Joshua, led them to the land.

Often we have trouble finding a vision of God's will in our lives because we have no experience in even knowing what to look for. The story of the Jewish people is one of needing a leader, a prophet, a guide. We encourage you to find such individuals in your life. You may be surprised to find that they can be ordinary people. They are people you look up to, feel safe with, trust, and are inspired by. Perhaps they will be people who have been through what you've been through and are farther down the road.

Vision also refers to God's face. We need to "see" that God is the only Parent who can truly meet our needs. As we experience our own emotional and spiritual loneliness, we discover that our human parents, spouses, and friends can not fill our deep voids for love and nurture. In recovery we seek to find intimacy and fellowship. Ultimately, we know that only a greater dependence on God will bring us the peace of knowing Him as *"Abba,* Father."[1]

As you search for your vision, your calling and direction, you may find that your pain is what informs you. You begin to find meaning in it. You've grown. You've experienced that more important than careers, money, status, and power are friendships, family, and your community. A day may come when you know you wouldn't exchange what you've gone through for anything. You begin to see that your pain let you discover what is really important. Now you may search for ways to help others know the peace you are finding. Paul's second letter to the Corinthians begins:

> Praise be to the God and Father of our Lord Jesus Christ, the Father of compassion and the God of all comfort, who comforts us in all our troubles, so that we can comfort those in any trouble with the comfort we ourselves have received from God. For just as the sufferings of Christ flow over into our lives, so also through Christ our comfort overflows. If we are distressed, it is for your comfort and salvation; if we are comforted, it is for your comfort, which produces in you patient endurance of the same sufferings we suffer *(1:3-6)*.

For this reason, we believe pastors who are in spiritual recovery for sexual sin and addiction can become much more effective pastors. They will be able to comfort and help others grow in ways in which they have been comforted and have grown.

This fact especially speaks to the question of restoration to ministry. Many denominations and church bodies exclude ministers from active ministry after they have "fallen" or committed sexual sin.

We believe we must make some distinctions about this. The key spiritually to whether or not a pastor can be restored to ministry is really his or her humility. If a pastor has been broken and is humble, he or she will be a much more effective pastor. If humility allows this person to seek help and to remain in accountability, he or she will be much less likely to sexually sin again than the average pastor. Humility and brokenness are two keys to safety.

In some situations, however, even such a pastor can't be restored to ministry directly. Legally the denominational authorities may not be able to restore this person if he or she has sexually abused a parishioner. This is because there is always the risk of the pastor committing another act of sexual misconduct. If the church authority knows about the history of abuse, and if the abuse reoccurs, the authority becomes liable for damage. Many religious authorities feel they are held hostage by this legal system.

Let us examine, however, why it might be important for a pastor not to return to active ministry, at least for a time, for positive reasons.

First, returning to ministry too quickly might not give the pastor enough time to heal emotionally and grow spiritually. A pastor in active ministry will start focusing on the needs of others and not of himself or herself.

Pastors will also need to focus on their families. The spouses of pastors who fall are often neglected when the pastors quickly return to ministry. The spouses are expected to forgive and forget and move on. This denies them the opportunity to work through their angers and hurts.

Children, of course, will also need to be attended to. Getting busy with ministry may not give the time necessary to focus on the healing journey.

Second, returning to ministry may not be fair to victims who have been damaged by sexual abuse. The knowledge that a pastor who has abused has now returned to ministry may further harm a victim. Knowing that pastor is in ministry may trigger memories in the victim's mind that will hurt him or her further. Victims and entire congregations that have been served by an offending pastor will need time to heal. When the pastor quickly returns to ministry, those who have been hurt may see this as an indication that their wounds were not taken seriously.

Any pastor or church leader should be held in accountability.

Third, many pastors have as much difficulty with their role as they do with sexual sin. They may be looking for affirmation from their role. They are dependent on the status it gives them. They have entered ministry for self-centered reasons. Taking time away from active ministry may help them evaluate their calling, too, and attitude about ministry.

Having said these things, we do believe that returning to ministry is possible for all who have committed sexual sin. We stand on Paul's words in Phil. 1:6, "that he who began a good work in you will carry it on to completion until the day of Christ Jesus."

When will a pastor be ready to return to ministry and not sexually sin again? We are all in danger of sexual sin regardless of our histories. We believe any pastor or church leader should be held in accountability.

Below is a short list of factors that are important to accountability and demonstrate safety:

1. Humility. This means a pastor has been honest about any history of sexual sin, perhaps not before the whole congregation, but certainly leadership should know of any problems.

2. Brokenness. A broken pastor will want to make amends to those he or she has harmed. Sometimes this can happen directly, sometimes not. "Amends" can mean simply changing behaviors so he or she won't repeat sinful ones. "Broken" means being willing to change and do the work to heal. Finally, "brokenness" means being willing to sacrifice one's lust and selfishness.

3. Fellowship. Pastors need to be in *intimate* fellowship—not just with one person but with a community of people. They will need to not be isolated.

4. Accountability. Pastors should have a written plan of how they will stay free of sexual sin. They should be aware of their rituals and acting-out behaviors. The plan should have defensive measures to avoid sin, and proactive measures for spiritual and emotional health. We have discussed the various important aspects of accountability in chapter 6.

5. Spirituality. Pastors should be in a process of spiritual direction in which they can demonstrate their active steps to grow closer with God. They should search for a vision and true calling.

6. Marriage. The pastoral couple should demonstrate how they are working to heal and grow their marriage into a greater one-flesh union. In all cases, the spouse will need to work equally hard on healing.

A pastor who wishes to return to active ministry should have a restoration "team" or committee. These people keep note of the pastor's ability to demonstrate healthy qualities of the factors listed above. This team should meet regularly and discuss how the pastor is doing. We have found that a pastor will be much more likely to remain in recovery if he or she is responsible to a group. Team members will all react differently to the pastor. When they meet to discuss, they will be much more likely to enforce healthy accountability.

This team should serve for at least a year. If the pastor has successfully demonstrated faithfulness during this time, as well as

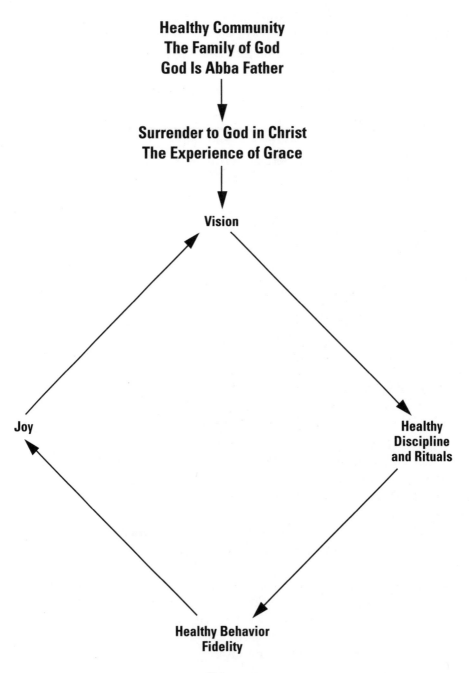

FIGURE 1
THE LAASER CYCLE OF RECOVERY

emotional and spiritual health, he or she may want to continue the accountability. In some ways we would encourage all pastors entering ministry to consider this plan to prevent possible problems. It is an act of humility to know that we need this kind of submission to authority. Many pastors object to the "severity" of such a plan, feeling their privacy is being violated. But we think that when a person seeks to serve in ministry, the responsibility he or she is taking is so grave they should be willing to commit to this submission.

> **God has redeemed our sins and experienced our pain.**

In chapter 1 we depicted the sexual addiction cycle first described by Dr. Patrick Carnes. Mark Laaser developed a cycle of health that substitutes healthy stages along the way instead of the unhealthy ones the addiction cycle presents. On the previous page is a diagram of what that looks like.

This healthy cycle begins with the spiritual acceptance of Christ. God has redeemed our sins and experienced our pain. We find healing for our emotions in the community of those mutually broken and dependent on God. This gives us a feeling of God's grace. We surrender to God's providential care. Grace produces a vision in us of where we would like to go, of how we would follow God's will in our lives. We see the face of God and know that the Father can fill our needs. Vision produces the energy to practice healthy rituals and discipline. Discipline produces healthy and faithful behavior. When we are faithful, we experience joy. Joy always stokes a vision, and the cycle repeats.

Pastors and others who replace the cycle of sexual sin with the cycle of growing dependence on God will truly be safe, healthy, and free of sexual sin.

Notes

Chapter 1

1. Both Mark Laaser and Ralph Earle have previously published books on sexual addiction. See the resource section for listings of those books.

2. Patrick Carnes, *Out of the Shadows* (Minneapolis: Comp Care Press, 1984), 4.

3. Patrick Carnes, *Don't Call It Love* (New York: Bantam, 1991), 127.

4. Carnes, *Out of the Shadows,* 15.

5. Carnes, *Don't Call It Love,* 93.

6. Ibid., 35. Carnes has a list of the percentages of addicts who have various other addictions.

7. For a more detailed description of the distinctions outlined in this chapter, see Mark Laaser and Nils Friberg, *Before the Fall* (Collegeville, Minn.: Liturgical Press, 1998), or Mark Laaser, "Sexual Misconduct Among Clergy: Update and Treatment Options," *Review and Exposition* 98, No. 2 (spring 2001).

8. John C. Gonsiorek, ed., *Breach of Trust* (Thousand Oaks, Calif.: Sage Publications, 1995), 145-54.

9. Glen Gabbard, "Psychotherapists Who Transgress Sexual Boundaries with Patients," in *Breach of Trust,* 135-44.

10. Marie Fortune, "Clergy Misconduct: Sexual Abuse in the Ministerial Relationship," in *Workshop Manual* (Seattle: Center for the Prevention of Sexual and Domestic Violence, 1992), 21.

11. Richard Irons and Katherine Roberts, "The Unhealed Wounder," in *Restoring the Soul of the Church*, ed. Mark Laaser and Nancy Hopkins (Collegeville, Minn.: Liturgical Press, 1995), 33-51.

Chapter 2

1. The reader who is more interested in a thorough treatment of boundaries and family systems would benefit from the work of David Olson; see, for example, Dean M. Gorall and David H. Olson, "Circumplex Model of Family Systems: Integrating Ethnic Diversity and Other Social Systems," in *Integrating Family Therapy,* ed. Richard H. Mikesell, Don-David Lusterman, and Susan H. McDaniel (Washington, D.C.: American Psychological Association, 1995).

2. See Mark Laaser's book *Talking to Your Kids About Sex* (Colorado Springs: Waterbrook, 1999).

Chapter 3

1. Mark Laaser, *Faithful and True: Sexual Integrity in a Fallen World* (Nashville: Lifeway Press, 1996), 171.

2. See the work of Ken Adams, *Silently Seduced* (Deerfield Beach, Fla.: Health Communication, 1991).

Chapter 4

1. The original design of these dimensions was created by Ginger Manley. See her article, "Healthy Sexuality: Stage III Recovery," *The Journal of Sexual Addiction/Compulsivity* 2, No. 3 (1995): 157-83.

Chapter 5

1. Theresa L. Crenshaw, M.D., *The Alchemy of Love and Lust* (New York: G. P. Putnam's Sons, 1996), 12.

2. Ed Wheat, M.D., and Gaye Wheat, *Intended for Pleasure* (Old Tappan, N.J.: Fleming H. Revell Co., 1977), 40.

3. Patrick Carnes, Ph.D., *Sexual Anorexia: Overcoming Sexual Self-Hatred* (Center City, Minn.: Hazelden, 1997), 138.

4. Howard Clinebell, Ph.D., *Counseling for Spiritually Empowered Wholeness: A Hope-Centered Approach* (New York: Haworth Pastoral Press, 1995), 18.

Chapter 7

1. Paxton Hibben, *Henry Ward Beecher: An American Portrait* (New York: Press of the Readers Club, 1942), 188-89.

2. Copyright 1988, Marilyn Murray.

3. Patrick Carnes, *The Betrayal Bond* (Deerfield Beach, Fla.: Health Communications, 1997), 26.

Chapter 8

1. Ralph Earle, *Come Here, Go Away: Stop Running from the Love You Want* (New York: Pocket Books, 1991), 29-48.

2. Carnes, *The Betrayal Bond*, 86.

3. Brenda Schaeffer, *Is It Love or Is It Addiction?* (Center City, Minn.: Hazelden, 1997), 4.

4. Patrick Carnes, Ph.D., David L. Delmonico, Ph.D., and Elizabeth Griffin, M.A., *In the Shadows of the Net: Breaking Free of Compulsive Online Sexual Behavior* (Center City, Minn.: Hazelden, 2001), 89.

5. Ibid., 42.

6. David Delmonico, Ph.D., Elizabeth Griffin, M.A., and Joseph Moriarity, *Cybersex Unhooked: A Workbook for Breaking Free of Compulsive Online Sexual Behavior* (Wickenburg, Ariz.: Gentle Path Press, 2001), 3.

7. David H. Olson and Amy K. Olson, *Empowering Couples: Building on Your Strengths* (St. Paul, Minn.: Life Innovations, 2000), 10.

8. Interpersonal Communication Programs, Inc., 30772 Southview Dr., Evergreen, CO 80439. Contact persons are Drs. Sherod and Phyllis Miller, at 800-328-5099.

9. Carnes, *Don't Call It Love*, 308.

Chapter 9

1. Carnes, *Don't Call It Love,* 109.
2. We actually heard Laurie Hall, author of the book *An Affair of the Mind,* tell this story at a conference.
3. This exercise is adapted from Mark Laaser, Deb Laaser, and Pat Carnes, *Open Hearts* (Wickenburg, Ariz.: Gentle Path Press, 1999).
4. Mark Laaser, *Faithful and True,* 63-65.
5. Mark Laaser, *Faithful and True,* 74-77.

Chapter 10

1. Brennan Manning's book *Abba's Child* (Colorado Springs: NavPress Publishing Group, 1994) and Sandy Wilson's book *Into Abba's Arms* (Wheaton, Ill.: Tyndale House Publishers, 1998) are great resources on this issue.

Resources

Books

Adams, Ken. *Silently Seduced*. Deerfield Beach, Fla.: Health Communications, 1991.

Aterburn, Stephen. *Every Man's Battle*. Colorado Springs: Waterbrook Press, 2000.

Carnes, Patrick. *Out of the Shadows*. Center City, Minn.: Hazelden, 2001.

_____. *Facing the Shadow*. Wickenburg, Ariz.: Gentle Path Press, 2001.

_____. *Don't Call It Love*. New York: Bantam Books, 1991.

Carnes, Patrick, Mark Laaser, and Debra Laaser. *Open Hearts*. Wickenburg, Ariz.: Gentle Path Press, 1999.

Carnes, Patrick, David L. Delmonico, and Elizabeth Griffin. *In the Shadows of the Net*. Center City, Minn.: Hazelden, 2001.

Clinebell, Howard. *Well Being*. San Francisco: HarperSanFrancisco, 1992.

Crenshaw, Theresa L. *The Alchemy of Love and Lust*. New York: G. P. Putnam's Sons, 1996.

Delmonico, David L., Elizabeth Griffin, and Joseph Moriarity. *Cybersex Unhooked*. Wickenburg, Ariz.: Gentle Path Press, 2001.

Dobson, James. *Life on the Edge*. Dallas: Word Publishing, 1995.

_____. *Love Must Be Tough*. Waco, Tex.: Word Books, 1983.

Earle, Ralph. *Come Here, Go Away*. Phoenix: Tri Star, 2000.

Earle, Ralph, and Gregory Crow. *Lonely All the Time*. Phoenix, Ariz.: Tri Star Visual Communications, 1998.

Earle, Ralph, and Marcus Earle. *Sex Addiction*. New York: Brunner/Mazel, 1995.

Laaser, Mark R. *Faithful and True: Sexual Integrity in a Fallen World*. Nashville: Lifeway Press, 1996.

_____. *Talking to Your Kids About Sex*. Colorado Springs: Waterbrook Press, 1999.

Laaser, Mark R. and Nancy Meyers Hopkins, eds. *Restoring the Soul of a Church*. Collegeville, Minn.: Liturgical Press, 1995.

Laaser, Mark R., and Nils Friberg. *Before the Fall*. Collegeville, Minn.: Liturgical Press, 1998.

London, H. B., and Neil B. Wiseman. *Pastors at Risk*. Wheaton, Ill.: Victor Books, 1993.

Lusterman, Don-David. *Infidelity*. Oakland, Calif.: New Harbinger Publications, 1998.

Murray, Marilyn. *Prisoner of Another War*. Berkeley, Calif.: PageMill Press, 1991.

Nouwen, Henri J. M. *The Return of the Prodigal Son*. New York: Image Books, 1992.

Roberts, Ted. *Pure Desire*. Ventura, Calif.: Regal Books, 1999.

Rutter, Peter. *Sex in the Forbidden Zone*. Los Angeles: Jeremy Tarche, 1989.

Schaeffer, Brenda. *Is It Love or Is It Addiction?* Center City, Minn.: Hazelden, 1997.

Schaumburg, Harry W., *False Intimacy*. Colorado Springs, Colo.: NavPress, 1997.

Schneider, Jennifer P., and Burt Schneider. *Sex, Lies, and Forgiveness*. Center City, Minn.: Hazelden, 1990.

Willingham, Russ. *Breaking Free*. Wheaton, Ill.: InterVarsity Press, 1998.

Audiotapes

Earle, Ralph, and H. B. London. *Pastors and Addiction*. Focus on the Family, 1999.

London, H. B. Pastor to Pastor Series, *Dangers of the Internet*. Focus on the Family, 2001.

_____. Pastor to Pastor Series, *Overcoming Sexual Addiction*. Focus on the Family, 1994.

National Directory Phone Numbers

New Hope Educational Foundation (Psychological Counseling Services, Ltd.)	(480-947-5739)
Faithful and True Ministries	(888-610-8094)
Sex Addicts Anonymous	(800-477-8191)
Sexaholics Anonymous	(615-331-6230)
Focus on the Family Pastoral Care Line	(877-233-4455)
American Association for Marriage and Family Therapy	(202-452-0109)
National Council on Sexual Addiction and Compulsivity	(770-541-9912)
American Association of Pastoral Counselors	(703-352-7725)
American Association of Christian Counselors	(800-526-8673)
Bethesda Workshops	(866-464-4325)

Websites

American Association of Christian Counselors	www.aacc.net
American Association for Marriage and Family Therapy	www.aamft.org
American Association of Pastoral Counselors	www.aapc.org
Bethesda Workshops	www.bethesdaworkshops.org
Faithful and True Ministries, Mark Laaser, Ph.D.	www.faithfulandtrueministries.com
Focus on the Family	www.pureintimacy.org
Focus on the Family, H. B. London	www.parsonage.org
Kid Shield	www.kidshield.com
National Association for Christian Recovery	www.christianrecovery.com
National Council on Sexual Addiction and Compulsivity	www.ncsac.org
Prodigals International	www.iprodigals.com
Psychological Counseling Services, Ltd., Ralph Earle, Ph.D. / New Hope Educational Foundation	www.pcs@pcsearle.com
Sex Addicts Anonymous	www.saa-recovery.org
Sexaholics Anonymous	www.sa.org

Praise for *The Pornography Trap*

"As we interact with pastors and laymen who contact us at Focus on the Family we are finding that one of the most debilitating addictions in this present age is that of pornography through print, film, and the Internet. Ralph and Mark have given us a weapon to combat this enormous social crisis. *The Pornography Trap* is a must for every Christian leader's library."

H. B. London
Vice President, Ministry Outreach/Pastoral Ministries
Focus on the Family

"Every struggling pastor or parishioner will discover the help they need in this useful resource. With clinical skill, Drs. Earle and Laaser guide readers on a path of hope, healing, and grace."

Rev. Dale O. Wolery
The Clergy Recovery Network

"This book goes beyond the damage done by pornography. It charters a new understanding of sexual health in a faith context. For all those who struggle with pornography, this book will be a relief, bringing new hope and understanding to partners as well."

Patrick J. Carnes, Ph.D., Certified Addictions Specialist,
Clinical Director of Sexual Disorders Services, The Meadows

"*The Pornography Trap* is a clear, concise, and comprehensive primer on sexual addiction. It is hard-hitting, yet empathic; realistic, yet forgiving."

Clifford L. Penner, Ph.D.
Coauthor of *The Gift of Sex*, *Restoring the Pleasure*, and *Men and Sex*

"Ralph Earle and Mark Laaser have produced a much-needed resource in *The Pornography Trap*. They discuss this threatening topic in a way that is realistic and hopeful, providing helpful information, provocative case studies, insights into the problem, and practical avenues of help."

Dr. John Huffman, Senior Minister
St. Andrews Presbyterian Church, Newport Beach, California

Defusing Pastoral Burnout

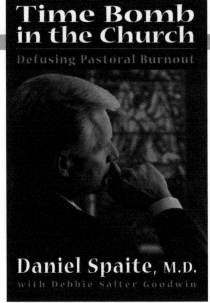

Time Bomb in the Church
Defusing Pastoral Burnout

Daniel Spaite, M.D.
with Debbie Salter Goodwin

For many pastors the fuse is slowly burning, getting shorter with every passing day. It's only a matter of time before the wear and tear of the pastorate explodes in the emotional and physical burnout, leaving only the charred fragments of a once vibrant ministry.

Among the rubble of raw emotion, broken families, and health problems, pastors find themselves trapped beneath the enormous weight of shepherding. Sunday comes seven days a week. And there is no relief in sight.

Physician Daniel Spaite and pastor's wife Debbie Salter Goodwin have written *Time Bomb in the Church* to help pastors identify harmful patterns of living that lead to burnout. Together, they provide expert advice on dealing emotionally and physically with one of the toughest jobs around. Overextended, exhausted, and exasperated pastors will find this book an encouragement in the search for balance in the midst of chaos. *Time Bomb in the Church: Defusing Pastoral Burnout*. Because pastors have personal lives too.